Hearings

on

INDIAN CLAIMS COMMISSION
H. R. 7837

bound with

Hearings

on

INDIAN CLAIMS COMMISSION
ACT
S. 2731

AMS PRESS
NEW YORK

COMMITTEE ON INDIAN AFFAIRS

WILL ROGERS, Oklahoma, *Chairman*

WILBURN CARTWRIGHT, Oklahoma
JOE L. SMITH, West Virginia
SAMUEL DICKSTEIN, New York
ROY E. AYERS, Montana
THOMAS O'MALLEY, Wisconsin
HENRY E. STUBBS, California
KNUTE HILL, Washington
ABE MURDOCK, Utah
THEO. B. WERNER, South Dakota
ISABELLA GREENWAY, Arizona
RANDOLPH CARPENTER, Kansas
JOHN STEVEN McGROARTY, California
ELMER J. RYAN, Minnesota
ANTHONY J. DIMOND, Alaska

FRED C. GILCHRIST, Iowa
SAM L. COLLINS, California
ISAAC H. DOUTRICH, Pennsylvania
FRED L. CRAWFORD, Michigan
J. GEORGE STEWART, Delaware
USHER L. BURDICK, North Dakota
BERNARD J. GEHRMANN, Wisconsin

DONALD B. JONES, *Assistant Clerk*

II

INDIAN CLAIMS COMMISSION

HEARINGS

BEFORE THE

COMMITTEE ON INDIAN AFFAIRS
HOUSE OF REPRESENTATIVES

SEVENTY-FOURTH CONGRESS

FIRST SESSION

ON

H. R. 7837

A BILL TO CREATE AN INDIAN CLAIMS COMMISSION,
TO PROVIDE FOR THE POWERS, DUTIES, AND
FUNCTIONS THEREOF, AND FOR OTHER
PURPOSES

———

MAY 22, 1935

United States. Congress. House. Committee on Indian Affairs. (handwritten)

UNITED STATES
GOVERNMENT PRINTING OFFICE
WASHINGTON : 1935

140548

Library of Congress Cataloging in Publication Data

United States. Congress. House. Committee on Indian
Affairs.
    Indian Claims Commission.

    Reprint of the 1935 ed. published by U. S. Govt. Print. Off.,
Washington.
    Issued with the reprint of the 1935 ed. of United States.
Congress. Senate. Committee on Indian Affairs. Indian Claims
Commission Act. New York [1976].
    1. United States. Indian Claims Commission.   2. Indians of
North America—Claims.   I. Title.
KF27.I45   1935b   343'.73'025   74-15122
ISBN 0-404-11982-4

Reprinted from an original in the collections
of the Ohio State University Libraries.
From the edition of 1935, Washington, D.C.
First AMS edition published in 1976

Manufactured in the United States

AMS PRESS, INC.
NEW YORK, N.Y.

INDEX

III

INDIAN CLAIMS COMMISSION

WEDNESDAY, MAY 22, 1935

House of Representatives,
Committee on Indian Affairs,
Washington, D. C.

The committee met at 10:30 a. m., Hon. Will Rogers (chairman) presiding.

The Chairman. The committee will please be in order.

By a vote of the committee at the meeting last Wednesday H. R. 7837 was set as special business for today. This is a bill to create an Indian Claims Commission, to provide for the powers, duties, and functions thereof, and for other purposes.

(The bill referred to is as follows):

[H. R. 7837, 74th Cong., 1st sess.]

A BILL To create an Indian Claims Commission, to provide for the powers, duties, and functions thereof, and for other purposes

Be it enacted by the Senate and House of Representatives of the United States of America in Congress assembled, That a Commission be and hereby is created and established, to be known as the " Indian Claims Commission ", which shall be composed of a Chief Commissioner and two Associate Commissioners, who shall be appointed by the President by and with the advice and consent of the Senate, The Commissioners shall continue in office during the existence of the Commission or until resignation or removal by the President only for inefficiency, neglect of duty, or malfeasance in office. Vacancies in the Commission shall be filled by the President in the same manner as original appointments. No vacancy shall interrupt the functioning of the Commission, nor impair the right of the remaining Commissioners to exercise all of its powers and to perform all its duties. The Commissioners shall not engage in any other business, vocation, or employment during their term of office. Each of the Commissioners shall receive an annual salary of $10.000, payable in the same manner as the salaries of judges of the courts of the United States.

Sec. 2. It shall be the duty of the Commission to investigate all claims against the United States of any Indian tribe, band, or other communal group of Indians residing within the territorial limits of the United States or Alaska, to ascertain and determine all of the facts relating thereto and all questions of mixed law and fact as may be incidental to such determination, and, on the basis of the facts found by it, to ascertain and determine the merits of all such claims, and to make findings with reference thereto. Such claims shall include all those whether sounding in contract or tort or otherwise with respect to which the claimant would have been entitled to redress in any court of the United States if the United States were subject to suit ; and all claims of whatsoever nature on account of any breach of duty committed by any officer or agent while purporting to act in the name or on behalf of the United States ; and all further claims under all treaties heretofore negotiated between the claimant and the United States but not formally ratified or executed by all of the parties thereto ; and those claims of whatsoever nature which would arise on a basis of fair and honorable dealings unaffected by rules of law and those which would result if the treaties, contracts, and agreements between the claimant and the United States were revised on the ground of fraud, duress,

1

or mutual or unilateral mistake whether of law or fact. Any such claim now pending in the Court of Claims, and any such claim previously referred by Congress to the Court of Claims and not yet filed in such court may be transferred, together with all the documents and certified copies of all the records relating thereto, by the complainant to the Commission at any time within the period provided for presentation of claims to the Commission, and all further proceedings with respect thereto shall be had under the provisions of this Act regardless of the terms of any Act giving jurisdiction of such claim to the Court of Claims. No claim shall be excluded because of the provisions of any other statute; nor because it has already been presented to the Congress; nor on the ground that it has become barred under any rule of law or equity, or by reason of any treaty or statute; nor on the ground of a prior adjudication with respect thereto in any judicial, administrative, or other proceeding between the same parties: *Provided, however,* That the Commission, when ascertaining the merits of any claim, shall take into consideration, and may inquire into, all previous adjudications or settlements of such claim and all payments made by the United States on its account. In any case wherein the Commission determines that a claim has merit under the provisions of this Act, the General Accounting Office and the Indian Office upon request of the Commission shall furnish such information as in the judgment of the Commission is required for the determination of set-offs.

SEC. 3. The Commission shall make a detailed report to the Congress of its findings of the facts of each claim, the conclusions reached as to the merits of such claim and the reasons therefor, together with an appropriate recommendation for action or nonaction by that body. If any claim shall be ascertained to be without merit in law or in fact, the Commission shall so report. If any claim shall be found to rest on some legal, equitable, or sound moral obligation, the recommendation shall be for a direct appropriation by the Congress in a specific amount, or for other adequate relief, or for the passage of an Act giving jurisdiction of such claim to the Court of Claims.

In all proceedings brought pursuant hereto in the Court of Claims all determination of fact by the Commission shall be accorded prima facie weight.

SEC. 4. The Commission shall be authorized to receive claims for a period of five years after the approval of this Act and no claim existing before such period not presented within such period may thereafter be submitted to any Federal court or administrative agency for consideration or action, nor will such claim be entertained by Congress.

Any claim within the provisions of this Act may be presented to the Commission by any member of members of an Indian tribe, band, or other communal group, as representative of all such members, regardless of the present status of such members as allottees, citizens, or unrestricted Indians; but wherever any tribal organization exists, recognized by the Secretary of the Interiod as having authority to represent such tribe, band, or group, such organization shall be accorded the exclusive privilege of representing such Indians, unless fraud, collusion, or laches on the part of such organization be shown to the satisfaction of the Commission.

SEC. 5. Immediately after its formation, the Commission shall send a written explanation of the provisions of this Act to the recognized head of each Indian tribe and band, and to any other communal groups of Indians existing as a distinct entity, and shall request that a detailed statement of all claims be sent to the Commission, together with the names of aged or invalid Indians from whom immediate depositions should be taken and a summary of their proposed testimony.

SEC. 6. The recognized representatives of each such tribe, band, or other communal group of Indians may retain to represent its interests in the presentation of claims before the commission an attorney at law, whose employment and the terms thereof shall be subject to the provisions of sections 2103, 2104, 2105, and 2106 of the Revised Statutes, and whose practice before the Commission shall be governed by rules and regulations hereby authorized to be formulated by the Commission. The Attorney General or his assistants shall represent the interests of the United States in connection with all matters pertaining to this Act.

SEC. 7. The Commission shall make a complete and thorough search for all evidence affecting such claims, utilizing all documents and records in the possession of the Court of Claims and the several Government bureaus and offices. The Commission or any of its members or authorized agents may hold hearings, examine witnesses, and take depositions in any place in the

United States and any of the commissioners may sign and issue subpenas for the appearance of witnesses and the production of documents from any place in the United States or Alaska, at any designated place of hearing. In case of disobedience to a subpena, the Commission may obtain an order from any court of the United States requiring obedience to that subpena; and any failure to obey such order shall be punished by such court as a contempt thereof. Witnesses subpenaed to testify before the Commission, witnesses whose depositions are taken pursuant to this Act, and the officers or persons taking the same, shall severally be entitled to the same fees and mileage as are paid for like services in the courts of the United States.

SEC. 8. The Commission shall give notice and an opportunity for a hearing to the interested parties before making any final determination upon any claim. A full written record shall be kept of all hearings and proceedings of the Commission and shall be open to inspection by the attorneys concerned. Whenever a final determination is reached by the Commission upon any claim, notice thereof shall be given to the tribe, band, or group concerned. Within twenty days thereafter written objections thereto may be filed with the Commission by any interested party. If such objections are not accepted by the Commission they shall be recorded as a part of the report on the claim presented to the Congress.

SEC. 9. The Commission may adopt all such rules for its own procedure, for the organization of its work, and for the effectuation of the purposes of this Act as it may deem appropriate. The Commission may employ and fix the terms of employment of such experts, field investigators, and professional and clerical assistants as may be necessary to fulfill duties which cannot be properly performed by persons already engaged in the Government service. At the Commission's request, the General Accounting Office, the Land Office, and the Bureau of Indian Affairs may transfer or temporarily assign to the Commission such of their employees as are specially qualified to assist the Commission in the performance of any of its duties under this Act.

SEC. 10. All necessary expenses of the Commission, including all reasonable traveling expenses incurred by the Commissioners, or under their orders, upon official business in any place outside the city of Washington, and including necessary expenses for suitable rooms and equipment for the principal office of the Commission in the city of Washington and for the performance of duty outside the city of Washington, shall be allowed and paid on the presentation of itemized vouchers therefor approved by the Chief Commissioner.

SEC. 11. Annual reports shall be submitted by the Commission to Congress showing the progress of its work. The Commission shall cease to exist on the fufillment of its duties under this Act; or, in any event unless extended by Act of Congress, on the expiration of ten years after the formal organization of the Commission. When the Commission shall cease to exist, all its books, documents, letters, official records, and other papers shall be transferred to the Indian Office.

SEC. 12. There is authorized to be appropriated for the purpose of carrying out the provisions of this Act such sums as the Congress may from time to time determine.

SEC. 13. This Act may be cited as the " Indian Claims Commission Act.'

The CHAIRMAN. The committee requested that the Departments interested in this legislation be invited to appear before this committee to advise us as to the necessity for this bill.

A report has been made by the Bureau of Indian Affairs of the Department of the Interior, but it is now being held up by the Bureau of the Budget and I would like to ask permission to insert that report in the record. We expect to receive same in a few days. If there is no objection, we will insert the report at this point.

(The report above referred to is as follows):

THE SECRETARY OF THE INTERIOR.
Washington, June 5, 1935.

HON. WILL ROGERS,
Chairman Committee on Indian Affairs,
House of Representatives.

MY DEAR MR. CHAIRMAN: Further reference is made to your request for report on H. R. 6655, a bill to create an Indian Claims Commission to investigate and determine the facts and the merits of all existing claims by Indian tribes against the United States, and to report its findings with appropriate recommendations to Congress. A series of conferences has been held since introduction of H. R. 6655, and as a result of these conferences text of the proposed legislation has been perfected and is now embodied in H. R. 7837 and S. 2731. Report is therefore being made on H. R. 7837.

The proposed commission, to be composed of three commissioners appointed by the President with the advice and consent of the Senate, is authorized to make a thorough search for all evidence on the facts involved in such claims, but may make determinations only after notice and hearing to all the interested parties. It is contemplated that the commission shall receive claims for a period of 5 years and that its work shall be completed within 10 years after its creation. It may report its recommendations to Congress as its determinations are made, and annual reports to Congress of the progress of its work are required.

The bill does not itself provide for the adjudication of any Indian claim. Its purpose is to expedite the handling of such claims, to provide Congress with competent, impartial advice on the disposition of the numerous requests by Indian tribes for the passage of jurisdictional acts or the allowance of appropriations, and to relieve the Court of Claims of the burden of highly complicated and necessarily prolonged fact determination.

Congress is now endlessly confronted with the challenge (a) to enact direct settlements with Indian tribes, and (b) to enact jurisdictional bills which more or less predetermine the ultimate settlement, in both cases without any adequate data upon which to reach a decision. Nor can this data be accumulated through legislative hearings in Washington. The immediate and, if necessary, sufficient justification of the pending bill lies in the above fact and in the way the bill would change that fact.

As a result of inadequate data the jurisdictional acts, among other peculiarities, often are inconsistent with one another, sometimes in the direction of leniency, and sometimes in the opposite direction, and in few or none of them are the authorizations and limitations based upon the particular and local history of the tribe and of its relations with the Government.

At present, after long preliminary negotiation and lobbying, eventuating in a jurisdictional act, a petition is filed in the Court of Claims, and the General Accounting Office goes through all records of expenditures, accumulating as certain or possible set-offs the detailed record of all the gratuitous expenditures for or in behalf of each tribe. The Indian Office, simultaneously or subsequently, prepares a lengthy history and discussion of the case. While the General Accounting Office is working on one case, many others are awaiting their turn, because much of the data is contained only in a single, unduplicated series of badly wornout records.

After many years spent in preparation the Government and the tribe go into combat before the Court of Claims under a jurisdictional act which usually is believed and admitted by all the parties to be inequitable, and which does not and should not have the character of an act for final settlement. Largely because of the unsatisfactory character of the acts, recovery in the Court of Claims by Indian tribes has become very infrequent, with resulting justifiable dissatisfaction by the tribes and their return to Congress for further redress.

The total operation is greatly influenced by elements of sheer accident, such as the possession by Indians of the wherewithal to hire attorneys for the initial lobbying of their case.

The above unsatisfactory state of affairs would be completely changed through the work of the commission under the pending bill. The commission would dispose of real and alleged claims, tribe by tribe. Its recommendations, whether for direct settlement or for jurisdictional acts, would be merely recommendations so far as Congress and the Budget were concerned, but its findings of fact would be a permanent accomplishment. The commission would be empowered and expected to take into account the particular historical circumstances of each tribe—its treaties and its land occupancy and its subsequent fate at the hands of the Government—and its present needs. In the ascertainment of set-offs, the commission would prepare for submission to Congress a total of possible set-offs such as in the commission's judgment may be fair in the light of the particular circumstances. In contrast to the present system, set-offs other than direct payments upon the claim need not be searched for except in the case of claims already determined to have merit, thus saving effort and expense. Furthermore, in ascertaining set-offs the commission would be in a position to prevent inequality of treatment by applying standards for the direction of research. Through photostating some of the records in the General Accounting Office, the commission would be able to dispose simultaneously of the set-off questions affecting numerous tribes. The commission would draw into its total picture the information in the possession of the Office of Indian Affairs—information which ordinarily, at present, is not put together until after a jurisdictional act, with all its fatalities, has become law.

Based upon the findings of fact and the recommendations of the commission, there undoubtedly will be many cases where Congress and the tribes can readily agree upon a direct final settlement, thus making unnecessary any litigation in the Court of Claims or the Supreme Court of the United States.

Where such direct settlement may prove to be not feasible because of unsettled legal questions, the claim may be submitted to the Court of Claims under an act framed on the basis of the research of the commission to present adequately all the issues requiring determination. As the findings of the commission are made prima facie evidence of the facts of the claim, further investigation of such facts is in most cases rendered unnecessary.

There will be no need of paying to private attorneys amounts which have aggregated millions, and which, before the final settlement is achieved under the now existing arrangement, would total tens of millions.

A somewhat increased cost to the Government (i. e. simply the expenses of the commission itself) will be balanced by a permanent reduction of costs in the Indian Office, the General Accounting Office, the Department of Justice, and the courts. And finally, it will be possible for the Indians, Congress, and the country to know with a clear conscience, that at least the facts have been ascertained and that the merits of the cases are set down in an adequate manner. It is believed that just, final settlement would follow as a matter of course.

I recommend enactment of H. R. 7837.

The Assistant Director of the Bureau of the Budget has advised that this bill "would not be in conflict with the financial program of the President, if section 3 were amended in accordance with the recommendation contained in the attached copy of the Attorney General's letter to me of May 24, 1935, and if section 9 were amended to provide that the employees of the Commission shall be subject to the provisions of the Classification Act of 1923, as amended."

To comply with the suggestion of the Assistant Director of the Budget, the words "subject to the provisions of the Classification Act of 1923, as amended", set off by commas, could be inserted on page 7, line 24, after the word "employ".

The amendment suggested by the Attorney General would be on page 4, line 25, to strike out the words "accorded prima facie weight" and to insert "admissible in evidence but may be reviewed by the court either on the basis of evidence taken before the Commission, or on additional evidence, or both."

Sincerely yours,

(Sgd.) HAROLD L. ICKES,
Secretary of the Interior.

The CHAIRMAN. Mr. Collier will make a statement concerning this bill.

STATEMENT OF HON. JOHN COLLIER. COMMISSIONER BUREAU OF INDIAN AFFAIRS, DEPARTMENT OF THE INTERIOR

Commissioner COLLIER. Mr. Chairman. I would suggest the great importance of the subject matter of this bill. This bill is an attempt to meet a recognized problem and a situation admitted to be unsatisfactory which has been before Congress and the Departments for many years.

I shall be exceedingly brief and will rather state the nature of the problem rather than indicate the details of the bill.

Ever since the beginning of the history of our Government in Indian affairs the Government has been entering into treaties with Indian tribes and having these treaties, either by agreement or unilateral action, and in later years supplementing them with agreements. Again, it has been acting as the guardian of the Indians in the absence of treaties. It has been recognizing the Indian title to areas of land, extinguishing the Indian claim of title to other areas, and having recognized title repeatedly the Government has changed its mind and altered and diminished them. The Government for a great many years has been the custodian of the Indian tribal trust moneys and has been using them in all kinds of ways.

Now, out of this total of the past record, extending down to this day, there have grown up innumerable grievances and claims, in some instances resting upon grounds which are definitely legal or ethical and therfore can be settled in the Court of Claims, that is, if they can get passed a jurisdictional act and if the act is drafted with a knowledge of the necessary facts then the case may be settled in the Court of Claims equitably.

A considerable number of the claims and grievances do not grow out of legal facts but essentially out of the moral parts of the record. There are a great many valid Indian claims, valid humanely and morally, but such have no basis in law. Now, year after year there appear before the Departments and the committees of Congress Indians and tribes of Indians petitioning for a settlement of their claims, either petitioning for jurisdictional acts to allow them to go into the Court of Claims or petitioning for some direct settlement or some adjustment which Congress can make without referring the matter to the Court of Claims.

There are many hundreds of tribes; there are actually more than 300 treaties not to mention the supplemental agreements and the number of claims is legion. Ne doubt many of these claims are fantastic, imaginary, but it is evident that a large number of them are valid because as years have gone on Congress has passed numerous jurisdictional acts and many cases have gone to trial in the Court of Claims and Congress also has enacted a considerable number of direct settlements.

Now in the first year of the preceding administration, the Wilbur-Rhoads administration, this matter was under serious strife and at that time the then Secretary of the Interior and the then Commissioner of Indian Affairs addressed a memorial to Congress pointing out all that I said today and in it they estimated that by the present method of disposing of these claims that at the present rate we could not hope to close the subject in less than 100 years. We believe the estimate of 100 years is far too optimistic and that centuries will have to be substituted for one century by the present rate and by the present method.

Now the effect is unsatisfactory all around. In the first place, it means that a large number of Indian claims that are valid in morals in every human sense never get considered at all. Scores, thousands of Indians and even whole tribes wait around decade after decade for a settlement and naturally they build up hopes of a golden age and the reaction upon their state of mind resulting from it is entirely bad. They do not get the settlement and they feel aggrieved, and they have a right to feel aggrieved.

The relationship between the Government and the Indians is made bad by the continuance of the situation. In the nature of the case committees of Congress cannot have a feeling of contact, they have not the facts on which to legislate and they do not get those facts at all adequately in the brief reports supplied by the proponents of the bills. The committees of Congress also cannot take the time to make the detailed examination needed to arrive at a sound and final conclusion.

Now the purport embodied in this bill is this, and I will just describe it in nonlegal and simple terms:

It is that Congress shall remand to a commission, or delegate to a commission, or vest in a commission the responsibility of fact-finding with respect to all of these claims of every kind and character. It will be limited only to tribal claims and not to individual claims. The latter are not dealt with in this bill.

It shall be the duty of this commission either to receive evidence or to go out and itself conduct an inquiry on the ground or in the records. As a fact-finding body the commission will reach conclusions, first, as to the existence of merit or lack of merit in a given claim, and having determined that there is merit in the claim it then proceeds to make a complete investigation which will include the assembly through the Comptroller's office and the Bureau of Indian Affairs the facts as to Government expenditures in behalf of that tribe, the data needed for the settlement of counterclaims or settlements.

Having completed its investigation the commission will report fully to Congress. It will report all of its findings to Congress and will accompany that report with a recommendation. The recommendation might be " no action " or the recommendation might be " a direct settlement " or some other adjustment of a gratuitous character, or it might be the enactment of a jurisdictional bill taking the whole matter into the Court of Claims.

Now, the bill provides that where a matter is referred into the Court of Claims after the commissioner has reported the fact-finding work of the commission shall be considered to have prima facie weight in the Court of Claims, thereby averting the need of retrying entirely these cases.

It is thought that by a method of this sort justice can be done and Congress can be enabled to do justice. You will note that the commission is not a court. It adjudicates nothing. It is only an agency of Congress ascertaining the facts, making recommendations but its findings of fact when the case goes to the Court of Claims have prima facie weight and will stand unless upset by competent evidence. That in a nutshell is the present bill.

Much work has been done by Mr. Poole, the Assistant Solicitor of the Department of the Interior and by Mr. Blair of the Department of Justice. They are both here and will be pleased to give you more technical information than I have tried to give you.

Mr. BLAIR. Of course, we realize that sometimes these claims are fantastic and potential and all that sort of thing. But what is the total of all these tribal claims that are now of record either by the introduction of bills or with petitions or other matters in your office?

Commissioner COLLIER. No man knows.

Mr. BLAIR. It runs into billions, doesn't it?

Commissioner COLLIER. The claims before the Court of Claims run to billions already, but if you take the claims that are pending and have not been sifted yet it is impossible to guess. I would not hazard a guess at $10,000,000 or $10,000,000,000.

Mr. BURDICK. It is about as much as we gave to the European countries isn't it?

Mr. BLAIR. It is probably more than that.

Commissioner COLLIER. It is impossible to guess. We are confident that there are many claims that are valid if not in law certainly in morals that are being pushed aside and procrastinated through lifetimes.

The CHAIRMAN. And it will be the business of this commission to ascertain which claims are legitimate claims and which are, as Mr. Blair has said, fantastic.

Commissioner COLLIER. The commission will work in the regular way; with sittings, or investigate in Washington. It will go on the ground and its procedure and its actions will all be of record and according to the rules that it would adopt.

Mr. GEHRMANN. Mr. Chairman, would not the statute of limitations be applied and include many of these?

Commissioner COLLIER. There is no statute of limitations there.

The CHAIRMAN. Have you any questions of the Commissioner?

Mr. BURDICK. I have no questions; he is not an expert.

Commissioner COLLIER. Thank you.

Mr. BLAIR. Oh, yes; why should not there be a statute of limitations?

Commissioner COLLIER. The statute of limitations does not run against the Government as a matter of law. It should not run against awards and the mere fact that something should have been done 40 or 50 years ago and was not done, and in the meantime the Indians were not able to get into the courts, should not bar them now.

Mr. BLAIR. I am in favor of giving the Indians full justice, but it will bankrupt the country to give it all.

Commissioner COLLIER. That will be for Congress to determine.

Mr. BLAIR. There should be some reasonable statute of limitations.

Commisioner COLLIER. Congress could adopt a rule of limitations instead of a statuate of limitations. Whatever this Commission does comes up to Congress with a full display of the facts with recommendation and Congress decides, except that now it decides without the facts and under pressure of a tribe that if they had enough money to get a lawyer to come here and work for it or under the pressure of a Department that likes a claim or to be skeptical about it.

The Indian Office is being continually required by the present system to present the claims on the basis of admittedly inadequate information. We are continually compelled to report adversely or favorably when we know we are not adequately informed.

Mr. GEHRMANN. There is one more question. Will these be final claims or are they only tribal claims?

Commissioner COLLIER. Individual claims are not involved here.

The CHAIRMAN. Does anyone else desire to ask any questions?

Mr. MURDOCK. I have a question, Mr. Chairman.

The CHAIRMAN. Mr. Murdock.

Mr. MURDOCK. Due to the fact that there is a question very vital to the Rocky Mountain group coming up, as chairman of that group I called a meeting this morning for 11 o'clock, and that meeting could not be postponed or I would have called it at another time, and so I would ask at this time that I be excused.

The Chairman. You may be excused.

Mr. Hill. I would like to ask this: Colonel Blair is here from the Department of Justice and Mr. Poole from the Interior Department. They have undoubtedly a prepared statement. I wonder if before we get the printed record whether we could get from Colonel Blair and Mr. Poole copies of their statements so that we might have the benefit of reading them over, as we will not be able to remain here any longer. If we can get such statements I know they will be very helpful to us.

Mr. Poole. We will be glad to furnish you copies of the statement.

Mr. Blair. I will also furnish statements and will be happy to do so.

The Chairman. Mr. Poole, of the Department of the Interior, will be the next witness.

Mr. Poole. Now, the statement that I have here is divided into two parts. The first part deals with the present situation, dealing with the Indian claims, and the second part with the provisions of the bill and how it is designed to meet those present defects.

Miss Westwood, from the Solicitor's office, is much better qualified to deal with that first part of the presentation, and I would like to defer that part of the statement to her and any questions that you have to ask on that, because I think she is in a position to give you some very valuable information.

The Chairman. Is she here?

Mr. Poole. Yes.

The Chairman. Do you want to go ahead with your testimony or would you prefer to wait and let Miss Westwood make her presentation?

Mr. Poole. I prefer to have Miss Westwood speak at this time.

The Chairman. Miss Westwood.

STATEMENT OF MISS CHARLOTTE WESTWOOD, OFFICE OF THE SOLICITOR, DEPARTMENT OF THE INTERIOR

Miss Westwood. Mr. Chairman, this report deals rather in detail with each step that is now undertaken in getting the claims to the Court of Claims, beginning with the presentation of the claim to Congress, and it is quite material when you consider the number of bills that are ordinarily introduced in Congress and the action that is taken upon them. As I have said, there are a great number of bills that are presented annually to Congress. I think within the last 3 or 4 years there have been 96 such bills. At the present session of Congress there have been presented 20 of these bills for jurisdictional action, and there were also presented 9 bills for amending unsatisfactory jurisdictional action. Very few of these bills ever get to Congress; and as is pretty well known, one of the reasons for that is that political backing is necessary to put these bills through; and the ascertainment of merit, as Commissioner Collier says, that has very little to do with it, because of the inability to get back of the situation. Last year, I believe, there was only one of such bills passed.

Now, we have investigations, particularly the Ballinger report, which made studies to the effect that a great deal of the expenditures were put upon the Indians in the initial stage in order to get up the material. The Department of the Interior and the Indian Office have frequently protested against the situation, because they are called upon to make a report dealing with each jurisdictional bill. It sometimes has a favorable report, and sometimes it has an unfavorable report, depending upon how the particular administration feels toward that particular claim. In several cases a bill comes up 10 or 12 times before Congress, and it will alternately receive favorable and unfavorable reports. Now, that is the first step.

Now, the second step is the bill itself.

The bill is usually inadequate. I mean, frequently it is inadequate for different reasons. In the first place, it cannot present to the Court of Claims certain questions. In a number of claims the Supreme Court has repeatedly said that the court has no power to alter or revise a treaty. A treaty is the supreme law of the land just like any law, and no court can make that law over again. It is only Congress that can do that; but a great many—I would not say the majority—but I believe a number of claims involve just that particular point, that the treaties were inequitable, they were made under misstatements of the facts or by misrepresentation; and so the Indian tribe gets its claim into the form of a jurisdictional act and goes through a long procedure of preparing the case for trial, only to have it dismissed on its merits in the Court of Claims, because the court says the court cannot decide the case, and it must go back again to Congress.

Well, with that limitation on the whole procedure, it is obvious that the Court of Claims can never decide this matter, and it is up to Congress to take care of the matter; and it is at this point that the commission would be of invaluable assistance, because, being a legislative arm of Congress, it can make those determinations as to whether there was a misrepresentation of the facts, or a misinterpretation, and inform Congress and settle the matter.

The second way in which a jurisdictional act is inadequate is that it has proven too often the Court of Claims is not acting on matters which the Indian tribe wishes to present. For example, it will be applicable on claims arising under any claims or laws. What the Indian tribe wants to have settled are matters arising from the duty of the guardian of the Indians, and the Court of Claims says that is not implied within the terms of the act; and under the old procedure, when it went to the Court of Claims, the Court of Claims would dismiss it. Well, that brings us to the presentation of the case for trial. I think it is fairly well admitted that this particular statute—you see, every judicial act, when the petition is filed under a jurisdictional act, the matter is immediately heard by the Department of Justice, and it goes to the Interior Department and the United States district attorney's office, and it calls for a statement of fact. Every claim, therefore, is permitted to have a statement of fact, regardless of whether it has merit or not, because it is up to the Court of Claims to decide the merit. Therefore, a great many claims go through the process of preparation, which takes a great deal of time, and many of them never should have been studied, because they have no merit, and of course, the Court of Claims will throw such cases out.

Of course, all claims need a thorough study, more or less, in order to discover whether they have merit or not; but a great many things are thoroughly out of the record, which will never be used. For example, if the claim is, we think, inadequate, if a claim cannot be recovered upon judgment, there is no reason to determine settlement in the claim, but the General Accounting Office is obliged to make long and detailed studies of the general accounting situation between the tribe and the United States.

At this point again the commission would be fairly desirable because it would require no determinations other than were necessary. No setoffs would have to be determined, and they would determine it upon its merit.

Five years ago the Senate committee investigating Indian affairs made a very thorough study of the situation and at the hearing it was brought out that the expense of these reports by the General Accounting Office were very great amounting in particular cases to $25,000 or $30,000, and if this expense could be eliminated in any considerable number of cases it would obviate and result in a great saving to the Government.

On the matter of the presentation of these cases it seems that on the average 10 years is required between the time the jurisdictional act is passed until the time the case is presented—I mean when the case is brought to trial in the Court of Claims.

After all this delay and expense you have the case at trial. Now, the hearings before the subcommittee seem to indicate that there is no discontent with the trial of the case itself in the Court of Claims. The preliminary steps are those which have to be corrected and it is at those that this Claims Commission bill is aimed. But after the trial of the case you have a very distinct situation that is very, very true of all claims where you are attempting to get a judgment in favor of an Indian tribe.

A computation recently was made and it seems that since 1930 out of 23 or so cases that had been decided only three have received any money judgments. The reason for that, of course, lies in the difficulty in the jurisdictional act which was mentioned before. Another very important reason is that the provisions are set off in the jurisdictional act.

It seems that Congress it quite inconsistent about applying gratuities. Sometimes they will require them to set off gratuities and sometimes they are not required to set off even a court claim by claim made upon a particular claim itself. Counterclaims usually refer to reimbursable projects of one sort or another. The result is that some bills are hopelessly handicapped at the very beginning and as time goes on the amount of money spent by the Government for the benefit of the Indians mounts up enormously until it would have to be exceedingly extravagant before the commission proposed in this bill could run up such expenses.

In five cases since 1930 the Court of Claims has said that the Indian tribes recovered and would have recovered a fairly adequate sum but in these five cases the claims had to be dismissed because there was the setoff—by the Government.

It was felt that a commission would also insist on this point because it can assure it some kind of standing in the determination of counterclaims by the Government applying an amount equally in all cases.

There were two points which might be raised in connection with this present Indian Claims Commission bill. One is on the subject of recovery. It was asked this morning as to whether there might not be very drastic recoveries against the United States bankrupting the Government. Well, as a matter of fact, even though the authorized commission itself might be extravagant the recovery even before 1930 was hardly a little bit more lenient. It amounted to hardly anything, to $50,000,000 or so on the claims that have been decided by the Court of Claims, and of that sum only about $18,000,000 had been recovered and it is felt that only a few million dollars will settle this whole matter of the Indian claims and may save the Government a great deal of expense not only in the presentation of cases but in the whole administration of the Indian affairs.

The second matter is the bringing up of claims. It might be said that a good many things might be brought which otherwise Congress or the Court of Claims should never have to settle. That is true to some extent because the whole purpose of the bill is to embrace all claims and get them out of the way as efficiently and as quickly as possible.

There is very little danger that things would be pushed forward by attorneys or other interested persons because of the necessity for contact in relation to claims in prosecution of claims to be approved by the Department of the Interior, and at that particular point it seems likely that many purely personal matters should be eliminated.

If there are any further questions I will endeavor to try to answer them.

The CHAIRMAN. Are there any questions which any members of the committee desire to ask the witness?

Mr. BURDICK. You have just given information. I want to get at the expert.

The CHAIRMAN. Are you through, Miss Westwood, or do you have something else?

Miss WESTWOOD. I am through for the present.

The CHAIRMAN. You may continue, Mr. Poole.

Mr. POOLE. Yes.

The CHAIRMAN. Miss Westwood is through for the present and we will now hear from Mr. Poole.

Mr. POOLE. Mr. Chairman, I take it that the committee is probably most interested in receiving an explanation of the bill at this time, and I will attempt to give in a rough way what this bill will provide.

Mr. BURDICK. Mr. Chairman, members of the committee understand this bill all right, but there are some parts of the bill to which there is objection and I think that those should be ironed out while the experts are here. Maybe if I would ask these questions to start with it might simplify the processes here. These claims are claims by Indian tribes against the Government. That is true, isn't it?

Mr. POOLE. Yes, sir.

Mr. BURDICK. This commission as set up is a Government commission to determine the facts?

Mr. POOLE. Precisely; it is an agency of Congress.

Mr. BURDICK. Did you ever hear of a case where the defendant in a law suit was allowed to find the facts and have those facts conclusive on the plaintiff? What right has this Government to set up a commission to determine facts which may be against the Government itself? Do I make myself clear or is it as confusing to you as it is to me?

Mr. POOLE. I am not certain what the Congressman has in mind.

Mr. BURDICK. All right, in line 6 of the bill——

The CHAIRMAN (interposing). What page is that?

Mr. BURDICK. On page 1, line 6, why don't you provide that at least one member of that commission should be an Indian? Why leave it to the white people who are being asked to determine the fact that the Indians want brought out? Why not put an Indian on it so that it will be at least an arbitration?

Miss WESTWOOD (interposing). The bill does not provide that. It says " the ' Indian Claims Commission ', which shall be composed of a chief commissioner and two associate commissioners, who shall be appointed by the President by and with the advice and consent of the Senate."

Commissioner COLLIER. I suppose you mean, Congressman, that in a given case an Indian representing the tribe which is presenting the claim.

Mr. BURDICK. I mean on the commission. I would like to have an Indian sitting on the commission.

Commissioner COLLIER. Wouldn't you want a man of the tribe interested? If a Sioux tribe a Sioux Indian, not an Indian in general, but an Indian representing the interests of that petitioning or litigating group.

Mr. BURDICK. I would be perfectly willing to have the one representing all of them, if satisfactory, but I think that is a defect of this bill to let a bunch of white men determine that matter.

Miss WESTWOOD. Doesn't the same thing happen to them in the Court of Claims?

The CHAIRMAN. Mr. Blair of the Justice Department would like to reply to the question of Congressman Burdick.

Mr. BLAIR. This is the situation: There have been no treaties made with the Indians since 1872. All of these claims arise from Government records. There is not any place to get them except from the records in the General Accounting Office and the records in the Department of the Interior. There is no verbal testimony in 99 percent of these claims. The determination of the merit of the case depends entirely upon Government records. Therefore that is the reason that we have furnished the testimony of what has been done and what is going on now. The Department of the Interior and the Comptroller General's Office furnish a statement of all transactions, correspondence, negotiations on record with the tribe at the time the treaties were made and signed. Those records after they have been filed are turned in to the Court of Claims, they are there available to the Indian tribes and to the courts and to the Government and it is on the basis of those records that these cases are to be tried so that the personnel of the commission could not possibly have very much standing. It is a determination like any other court determination based upon recorded facts.

Mr. BURDICK. When you get all through, this commission that makes the report to the Court of Claims, it does not mean anything except that it is a prima facie statement of the facts by the commission and you go over that statement of the commission and find other facts under the terms of this bill. Then the commission would from the facts obtained from the records of the Comptroller General's Office and the Interior Department records report to the Congress whether or not in the judgment of the commission it was a meritorious claim and based either in law or equity or upon fair dealing. The Court of Claims can take the findings of fact of the commission.

Mr. BLAIR. Like any other court they will consider the findings.

Mr. BURDICK (reading):

In all proceedings brought pursuant hereto in the Court of Claims all determinations of facts by the commission shall be accorded prima facie weight.

That means it is there but it can be disputed and overcome.

Mr. BLAIR. Practically all courts can overrule the findings of any special master. Any court can overrule the findings of the jury.

Mr. BURDICK. Then if they have the power to overrule the facts wouldn't it be fair to the Indians to have an Indian sitting on the commission when those facts are found?

Mr. BLAIR. I have no objection to it.

Mr. BURDICK. I have a special reason to believe that it will help.

Mr. BLAIR. That is a matter for Congress.

Mr. DIMOND. Mr. Chairman, I would like to ask a few questions.

The CHAIRMAN. Mr. Dimond.

Mr. DIMOND. Mr. Chairman, is there any substantial reason why an Indian should not be a member of this commission since it is perfectly plain that there are plenty of Indians who are capable enough to do this job and why not put them on. I think it would be a very wise thing to do——

Mr. POOLE (interposing). I was wondering, Mr. Congressman, that inasmuch as this body really acted for Congress whether Congress would not be more satisfied if they were impartially constituted. Now, if one of the members or 2 or 3 of the members or all of the membership were made up of Indians, it strikes me that you might not get such a decision in any case.

Mr. BURDICK. I do not get your point there.

Commissioner COLLIER (interposing). I rather like the Congressman's idea. There are plenty of Indians who are qualified and it might be specified that one of the commissioners shall be an Indian. It might be mentioned in this fashion " * * * of whom one shall be an Indian."

Mr. BURDICK. " * * * of whom one at least shall be an Indian."

The CHAIRMAN. I think, Mr. Burdick, that it would be perfectly agreeable to so amend the bill if the committee sees fit to comply with your suggestion.

Mr. BURDICK. There is another suggestion that I would like to make; that is, in section 10 it provides—

All necessary expenses of the commission, including all reasonable traveling expenses incurred by the commissioners, or under their orders, upon official business in any place outside the city of Washington, and including necessary expenses for suitable rooms and equipment for the principal office of the commission in the city of Washington and for the performance of duty outside the city of Washington, shall be allowed and paid on the presentation of itemized vouchers therefor approved by the chief commissioner.

Out of what fund will this be paid?

Mr. Poole. In section 12 it provides—

there is authorized to be appropriated for the purpose of carrying out the provisions of this act such sums as the Congress may from time to time determine.

According to that section there is authority for Congress to appropriate funds for the purpose of carrying out the provisions of the act.

Mr. Burdick. Does it contemplate the appropriation of trust funds of the Indians?

Mr. Poole. No, sir; it does not, from the Treasury of the United States.

The Chairman. Does anyone else desire to ask any questions?

Mr. Dimond. Mr. Chairman, I have just one more question.

The Chairman. Mr. Dimond.

Mr. Dimond. Section 6 provides—

the recognized representatives of each such tribe, band, or other communal group of Indians may retain to represent its interests in the presentation of claims before the commission an attorney-at-law, whose employment and the terms thereof shall be subject to the provisions of sections 2103, 2104, 2105, and 2106 of the Revised Statutes, and whose practice before the commission shall be governed by rules and regulations hereby authorized to be formulated by the commission. * * *

I think we are always on dangerous ground when we permit any commission to start making rules and regulations. We might write them in the bill itself. If left to them they might decide that no one practicing law outside of the District of Columbia might practice before them.

The Chairman. You are referring to section 6, line 8?

Mr. Dimond. Yes, sir; particularly to line 8 of section 6.

Commissioner Collier. It says "whose employment and the terms thereof shall be subject to the provisions—of the various sections of the existing law" which would mean that any tribe or group of Indians could pick a lawyer to represent their interests.

Mr. Dimond. But it provides—

and whose practice before the commission shall be governed by rules and regulations hereby authorized to the formulated by the commission.

I think it would be better to say " and the practice shall be * * * in accordance with the rules and regulations " and then it will be within the power of the Court of Appeals to authorize rules and regulations.

Mr. Blair. I would suggest this, that probably the reason for that suggestion in the bill was this: The Interstate Commerce Commission has rules and regulations for attorneys practicing before it. So does the Bureau of Internal Revenue. So do several of the departments which have rules and regulations governing who shall be admitted to practice before them. It has been found, according to my information, that that is very necessary, otherwise attorneys would come in there who do not measure up to the standards that ought to be for such practices. The same thing is true of this commission as any other commission or body.

Mr. POOLE. What would you do, Congressman, if an attorney was contemptuous? If he was before a court they would have the right to disbar him or keep him from practicing before it.

Mr. BURDICK. Well I would suggest that you make the rules and regulations apply to everybody and not pick out any individuals.

Mr. POOLE. I think the language of this section contemplates that.

Mr. BURDICK. You ask Commissioner Collier about the English.

Commissioner COLLIER. I think the word " practice " covers it perfectly or the words " the practice " will cover it.

The CHAIRMAN. Is there any further questioning? If not, we will have Mr. Poole make his statement.

Mr. POOLE. If there are no further questions, I will read the statement that I have prepared.

The CHAIRMAN. All right; if there are any other questions they can come later.

Mr. BURDICK. I have not as yet examined the expert.

STATEMENT OF RUFUS G. POOLE, ASSISTANT SOLICITOR, DEPARTMENT OF THE INTERIOR

Mr. POOLE. Mr. Chairman and gentlemen: My statement as to this bill on the proposed Indian Claims Commission, H. R. 7837, is as follows. It was introduced on May 1, 1935, and it would, if enacted, establish an Indian Claims Commission with the purpose of achieving a rapid, final, and just disposition of all outstanding Indian claims against the Government. The Commission, composed of three commissioners appointed by the President with the advice and consent of the Senate, would perform four major functions:

First. The investigation of existing Indian claims;

Second. The determination of all facts relating thereto;

Third. The ascertainment of the merits of the claims; and,

Fourth. The report to Congress of the facts and the merits of the claims with specific recommendations for the settlement of meritorious claims or for a jurisdictional act to transfer meritorious claims which involve disputed legal questions to the Court of Claims

The reasons which make this bill important may be discussed under three major headings:

I. The necessity for prompt and just disposition of Indian claims,

II. The inadequacy of the present method of disposing of Indian claims, and

III. The remedy offered by the proposed claims commission.

I. THE NECESSITY FOR PROMPT AND JUST DISPOSITION OF INDIAN CLAIMS

Investigators of Indian affairs and successive commissioners have insisted that the Government's administration of Indian affairs is in a large measure ineffective and futile so long as the tribes have claims against the Government which they believe to be just. The Meriam study of The Problem of Indian Administration (1928) expressly finds that—

The existence of these claims is a serious impediment to progress. The Indians look forward to getting vast sums from these claims; thus their economic future is uncertain. They will hardly knuckle down to work while they still hope the Government will pay what they believe is due them [page 19]. The disturbing influence of outside agitators seeking personal emoluments and the conviction in the Indian mind that justice is denied, renders extremely difficult any cooperation between the Government and its Indian wards [page 805].

At the hearings held 5 years ago by the subcommittee of the Senate Committee on Indians Affairs for the purpose of investigating the problem of the slowness of the prosecution of Indian claims, the settlement of these claims was accepted by the Senators and by the Indian commissioners as a fundamental need. (See Survey of Conditions of the Indians in the United States pt. 25, Hearings, hereinafter referred to simply as " hearings ", 72d Congress, 1st session, Jan. 22, 1930, at 13410 et seq. See also the testimony of Commissioner Meritt at the hearings before the subcommittee of the House Committee on Indians Affairs on the appropriation bill for 1914, at 99; and to the same effect the Annual Report of the Secretary of the Interior, 1934 at 83.

Furthermore, the present method of handling those claims which have received attention only aggravates the situation since, as will be demonstrated in some detail, it postpones their settlement an almost indefinite time, and in the meanwhile wastes the substance of the claimants and puts the Government to heavy expense, and results mainly in disappointment and unjustified defeat.

II. INADEQUACY OF THE PRESENT METHOD OF DISPOSING OF INDIAN CLAIMS

No solution of the problem is promised by the present system which not only is highly inefficient in functioning but fails to accomplish its task of settling Indian claims and settling them justly. The system was investigated by the subcommittee of the Senate Committee on Indian Affairs in 1930 and many of its deficiencies were then disclosed. Drawing upon the facts presented to that subcommittee and upon information available from other Government records and other studies of the situation, an analysis can be made of each step in the present process of settling a claim, revealing the defects which make the whole process slow, expensive, and fruitless.

By way of summary, it may be said at this point that the process is slow because it normally takes several years and much lobbying to secure a jurisdictional act, and because, on the average, 10 years then pass before the claim comes to trial. It is also expensive for these reasons plus the fact that much of the labor is unnecessary. And it can be termed fruitless because 21 of the 24 cases decided since 1930 were dismissed, and of these 21 at least 5 and probably more were dismissed because an otherwise valid recovery was submerged by a preposterous system of set-offs. The slowness of the system can be indicated by the fact that about 70 of the petitions filed in the Court of Claims which had been pending for many years at the time of the subcommittee investigation in 1930 are still pending. It is true that the disposition of cases which was just over one a year before 1930 has increased to just over five a year since then; one reason for this increase is that many of the extensive and complicated accounting reports which had required 3 to 5 years of the General Accounting Office's time and probably cost in some instances $25,000 apiece were completed fairly recently. The slowness of the system may also be indicated by the fact that the 24 cases which have been decided since 1930 have required on the average 8½ years from the time Congress assented to their suits until their decision. Today there are 98 petitions pending in the Court of Claims.

The number of claims which still seek settlement, besides these 98 now pending, including those that come back to Congress after unsatisfactory treatment and those which have not yet been presented to Congress cannot be estimated. Suffice it to point out that since the first session of the Sixty-ninth Congress, 96 bills have been presented which Congress did not act upon. At the present rate of progress, there would appear to be more than one century ahead of troublesome Indian claims.

Better than by summary statistics, the defects of the present system can be demonstrated by an analysis of the functioning of its several processes.

First, presenting the claim. The first step is getting the claim before Congress. Here some tribes are baffled, not sure how to make definite and press their claims (see the statements and questions of Indians about the claims of their tribes made to the subcommittee of the Senate Indian Affairs Committee taking testimony in various western States, hearings, at 13609–13670), and others are the victims of self-seeking attorneys. Even normally, however, the success which a tribe has in getting its case before Congress depends on such irrelevant matters to the merits of its case as its wherewithal to employ the necessary investigators and attorneys and its sophistication in doing so.

Second, securing the jurisdictional act. Perhaps the most disheartening of all the various labors in pushing a claim is the work of securing a jurisdictional act.

In regard to volume of bills: In less harassed congressional sessions than the present a great many of these jurisdictional bills flood in, all presenting peculiar and complicated fact situations which in only a very few situations can a committee adequately study. In 1930 there were 49 such bills before the Congress (see letter of Senator Thomas to the Attorney General, hearings, at 13526) ; there were at least 25 presented to the Seventy-third Congress. The present Congress is burdened with 20 original and 9 amendatory bills. But these bills are persistent plaintiffs and return session after session despite disregard, defeat, and veto and regardless of whether they are meritorious or not. For example, since the first session of the Sixty-ninth Congress, the Oregon Indians have presented their claims nine times and the Colville and Okanogan Indians six times.

In regard to political considerations: The few bills which are finally passed are those fortunate enough to secure correct political backing, often regardless of the merits of the claim. Admittedly political considerations dominate in a situation which should be governed solely by judicial considerations.

Much depends upon the standing in Congress of the sponsors of the bill, upon the composition of the Committees on Indian Affairs, and upon the attitude of the administration (Meriam Report, op. cit. supra, at 805–806).

The attitude of the administration is one of the variable and political elements not only because of the possibility of a veto but because of the fact that each jurisdictional bill is sent to the Interior Department for a report. The bill which repeatedly comes before Congress may receive sometimes a favorable and sometimes an unfavorable report; for example, in the case of the jurisdictional bills for the California Indians, within 6 years, they received twice favorable and twice unfavorable reports. (See Meriam, op. cit. supra, at 806.) A somewhat similar fate befell the bills for the Iowa Indians in spite of a fairly careful study and endorsement of the claim by the House Indian Affairs Committee only the second time the bill was presented. (See S. Rept. 303, 64th Cong., 1st sess., Mar. 25, 1916, incorporating H. Rept. 1398, 62d Cong., 3d sess.) The Indian Office and the Interior Department have many times protested against this reference of jurisdictional bills to them for report, contending that as they are obligated to be the special guardian and chief friend of the Indian, and as many of the claims are founded on alleged administrative errors in the more or less remote past, it is frequently inappropriate and difficult to make such decision. (See Hearings, at 13410.)

In regard to expense and delay:

> The result is that before a jurisdictional act is finally secured many years must frequently be consumed in agitation, propaganda and lobbying. (Meriam, op. cit. supra, at 806.)

The Indian claimants must meet the expense of attorneys, representatives, witnesses, delays and defeats, and often, of trying their case twice, once before the committee and once before the Court of Claims. As supporter of the Indians the Government must ultimately meet this same expense as well as the expense of the continuous delay and harassment of Congress. Obviously this cost to the Government of this blind repetitious process is enormous.

Third, insufficiency of the jurisdictional act. Further waste attendant upon the system is the passage of stillborn acts, acts which can bring the claimants little or no benefit. This grows out of the fact that Congress is an inappropriate body to pass upon Indian claims without having responsible impartial advice.

Constitutional inability to confer jurisdiction: In one case, that of the Turtle Mountain Chippewa, the jurisdictional bill had been presented five times to Congress. Finally in 1933 it was passed, only to be vetoed; and was repassed in 1934, again only to be vetoed. It is now again before Congress in another form. The veto rested on the fact that the claim in effect demands the reformation of a treaty—a thing the Court of Claims cannot and will not do. (*Sisseton and Wahpeton Indians* v. *United States*, 58 Court of Claims at 302 (1923); affirmed, *Sisseton and Wahpeton Indians* v. *United States*, 277 U. S. at 424 (1928).) Despite this fundamental objection the claim will continually be pressed before Congress and because it appeals to the sense of justice, may finally be given a jurisdictional act only to be dismissed from the Court of Claims 10 or 20 years later after arduous work by the General Accounting Office, the Indian Office, the Department of Justice, and the attorneys for the Indians.

Congress does not appear to learn that a great many claims cannot be settled by the Court of Claims but only by political action, in spite of the fact that all the many claims which sought relief from fraud, duress, or mistake of fact and which have been sent to the Court of Claims were dismissed for want of jurisdiction. The court repeatedly said, first, that the stereotype language of the jurisdictional act regularly employed, " all claims arising under any treaty ", did not permit consideration of claims attacking rather than relying on the treaty, and, secondly, that in any event the reformation of treaties was a political function which Congress could not constitutionally place upon the judicial branch. (*Otoe and Missouria Indians* v. *United States*, 52 Court of Claims at 424 (1917) (claim based on inadequate consideration for treaty cession); *Sisseton and Wahpeton Indians* v. *United States*, 58 Court of Claims at 302 (1923) (claim based on mistake and misrepresentation as to the acreage ceded by treaty); *Creek Nation* v. *United States*, 63 Court of Claims at 270 (1927) (claim for value of land ceded without consideration and because of duress); *Osage Tribe of Indians* v. *United States*, 66 Court of Claims at 64 (1928) (claim for proceeds of sale of land because of inability to understand the words of the treaty).) The doctrine has firm roots in Supreme Court decisions. (*United States* v. *Old Settlers*, 148 U. S. 427 (1893); *United States* v. *Chictaw, etc. Nations*, 179 U. S. 494 (1900); *Sisseton and Wahpeton Indians* v. *United States*, 277 U. S. 424 (1928).) It must be noted that if the treaties in these cases had been contracts between ordinary individuals, in most of them, if complete evidence had been allowed, an equity court would have allowed reformation, so that the claims in these cases can be considered " merely moral " only because they relate to treaties. In the *Osage case, supra*, even a law court might well have doubted whether there were any contract as there obviously occurred no " meeting of the minds." Moreover, the Court of Claims is inclined to consider itself as helpless to reform agreements between the United States and the Indians as treaties. (See *Klamath and Moadoc Etc. Indians* v. *United States*, E. 346 (Apr. 8, 1935) at 12. But compare *Iowa Tribe of Indians* v. *United States*, 68 Court of Claims at 585 (1920) (recovery of additional compensation based upon an oral agreement).) In this *Iowa case* the court was influenced by the unusually broad and explicit language of the jurisdictional act.

As to the inadequate language in the acts: Although in a great many cases the language of the jurisdictional act is decisive of the claim, the language is often deficient not only in the way previously discussed, but sometimes because it is restricted to specific claims under specific treaties (compare Ute Indian Act of Mar. 3, 1909, 35 Stat. 788) or too broad (compare Sioux Indian Act of June 3, 1920, 41 Stat. 738, all " amounts, if any, due said tribe from the United States * * * ") or does not cover the type of claim which the tribe has (compare *Choctaw and Chickasaw Nation* v. *United States*, 75 C. Cls. 494). The reason is that the acts do not reflect the history of the tribe and cannot do so as long as they must lack the study which should attend them.

In regard to the irrationality of the set-off provisions: The greatest injustice done by the jurisdictional acts is, however, the utterly inconsistent and irrational provisions for set-off. Some acts will provide simply for set-off of payments made upon the claim, others will allow also for set-off of counter claims, as in the act founding the Creek claims, May 24, 1924 (43 Stat. 139), which are usually the unpaid parts of reimbursable agreements, but the most devastating of all is the increasingly frequent allowances in acts of set-off of gratuities. Congress has shown a strange partiality in the infliction of this provision. It has usually avoided placing it in the jurisdictional acts for the Five Civilized Tribes.

The set-off of gratuities means that all money ever spent by the United States in any way for the benefit of the tribe may be deducted by the court from the recovery won by the tribe. Because the matter can be settled only piecemeal in court, neither the Department of Justice nor the General Accounting Office has any definite or consistent standard as to what is for the benefit of the tribe. (Hearings, at 13418.) As a result none of the parties can gage the strength of his case. When the General Accounting Office reports a gratuity set-off so large that recovery appears to be out of the question, the lawyer for the claimants does not end the case as he does not know how many of the items included in the report the Department of Justice and the Court of Claims will reject as not appropriately deducted as gratuities; or he may seek an amendment of the jurisdictional act to strike out set-off of gratuities. This was the dilemma that confronted the lawyer in the Klamath general accounting cases, E–350 (reported out of the General Accounting Office in 1928, and apparently not yet decided; Hearings at 13480, 13481.)

The, shocking inconsistency in the various holdings of the Court of Claims as to what may be deducted from the recovery won by the tribe as a gratuity may be illustrated by the following citations. Sometimes the Court of Claims allows the Government set-off for educating the tribe's children in nonreservation Indian schools. (*The Blackfeet, Blood, et cetera, Tribes* v. *The United States*, E–427, Apr. 8, 1935) and sometimes it does not (*Fort Berthold Indians* v. *United States*, 71 C. Cls. 308). More fatal to recovery is the allowance of a set-off of all the money the Government has spent in the administration of Government agencies, as for superintendents, interpreters, teachers, Indian police, agency buildings, and so forth. (*The Duwamish, Lumme, et cetera, Tribes* v. *The United States*, F–275, June 4, 1934), on the ground that these things are benefits to the Indians. But in another case the court said it should exclude such items recognizing that the maintenance of a Government agency is simply the performance of a governmental function and an obligation incurred by the United States in developing the reservation policy; and furthermore that such expenditures are common expenditures for all tribes. (*The Assiniboine Tribe* v. *The Unites*, J–31, Apr. 10, 1933.) Sometimes the court has realized that this argument should exclude set-offs for money expended for education and civilization, but normally the court allows deduction even for this. (*The Duwamish, Lummi, et cetera, Tribes* v. *The United States, supra; The Crow Nation* v. *The United States, supra.*) Sometimes the court does not bother to analyze and reject erroneous deductions in the accounting prepared by the General Accounting Office saying that the total set-off is so large that the Indian tribe has no hope of recovery anyway. (*The Crow Nation* v. *The United States, supra.*)

Result: The deduction for money which obviously the Government would have spent and has spent for all tribes not only is grossly unfair to the tribes with just claims against the Government for wrongs done them by the Government, but it has resulted in the fact that since 1929 in every case but two where the jurisdictional act allowed off-set of gratuities and where a recovery has been won in the court the petition has been dismissed because the recovery was exceeded by the set-offs.

Could anything be so wasteful or so futile in fulfilling its purpose of quieting Indian claims as the continuous dismissal of just and proven claims either because the court has no jurisdiction of them or because the recovery is blotted out by the Government? It is obvious that if this policy is continued it will be more and more hopeless for the Indians to sue the Government except on very extravagant claims, for the amount of the Government expenditures in carrying out its Indian policies is increasing enormously daily.

The result of inadequate jurisdictional acts is that after an act is passed, the claimant returns for amendments. Probably more than half the acts passed have been subjected to amendments. Far more wasteful than this result is, however, the lack of finality which must result when a just claim has not been given justice in the Court of Claims, either because of rules of law or otherwise. Congress is constantly being petitioned for new acts for the benefit of claims which have been decided in the Court of Claims. (See for example, the Otoe and Missuoria bill (S. 2560) and the Stockbridge and Munsee bill (H. R. 5230) now before Congress and each introduced twice before), and occasionally Congress grants the request (see *Delaware Tribe* v. *United States*, 72 C. Cls. 525 (1931)), and the whole wasteful process of preparation begins again.

Fourth, preparation of the case: The unsatisfactory features of the present system do not end with the defective jurisdictional acts. The practice is for the Department of Justice upon receipt of the tribe's petition after its filing in the Court of Claims to send copies of the petition with a form letter to the Department of the Interior and to the General Accounting Office. Since the Department of Justice is naturally uninformed of the facts of the claim, the form letter can contain no analysis of the petition and no instructions as to the information desired; it simply requests all the information which the Interior Department or the Office may have on the subject. "Hearings", at 13522, 13577. Inevitably a very great deal of time, even many years, is wasted in the accumulation by the Department and especially the General Accounting Office of a mass of material which later is found to be unnecessary and irrelevant. "Hearings", at 13494, 13499. Furthermore, many of the cases arise from the action of the Government in dealing with land which has no relation to the books of account and do not require accounting. Thus, in the Osage case, there was nothing but a question of law and it was decided on that basis (66 Court of Claims at 69), but the case had to be delayed for about 4 or 5 years for reports costing, as was estimated, about $25,000 or $30,000. "Hearings", at 13522.

This was the situation in 1930 and it may have improved since then, but certain inherent defects cannot be removed or improved under the present system. These defects lie in the fact that every petition no matter how patently or latently worthless on its facts, if it is not dismissed on a point of law on demurrer, causes years of search not only into the facts, but at the same time into all the possible set-offs and defenses. This means that every claim, particularly where other set-offs are allowed than simply payments upon the claim, is held up for the 2 or 10 years which is necessary to do a general accounting of all financial matters between the Government and the tribe sometimes as far back as 1789, although such set-offs might never be needed because the claim could be dismissed as worthless on the facts. This defect is due to the fact that because of the nature of a judicial trial both sides must be ready on all points at the same time. The inappropriateness of trying to settle Indian claims indiscriminately by trial before the Court of Claims is apparent from this one fact alone.

Fifth, trial of the case: There are no complaints about the administrative efficiency of the Court of Claims. Indian claims when ready for trial receive prompt attention. Informed and interested persons have always denied that the notorious delay in the disposal of Indian claims was due to crowded dockets or congestion in the court itself. " Hearings ", at 13413. For this reason the solution of the Indian claims problem proposed in 1930 in H. R. 7963, namely the creation of a separate court of indian claims, was officially rejected by the Department of the Interior and the Department of Justice and instead amendments to the bill or alternative proposals were suggested to set up a claim-sifting commission on the order of that proposed herein. Congressional Record June 27, 1930, at 11901 et seq.; letter of Attorney General Mitchell to the Director of the Bureau of the Budget, March 11, 1930.

Sixth, failure of recovery: The extravagant effort and expense that the Government and the Indians have put into the disposition of Indian claims have brought little good to the Indians especially in recent years. Of those claims which were really meritorious and deserved attention and which worked their way to the Court of Claims, some were dismissed because the court denied jurisdiction of the substance of their claim, some were dismissed because the language of the jurisdictional act was unfortunately drawn, and some were dismissed because the set-offs wiped out the recovery. This last reason has played a more and more prominent role because of the increasing frequency of the appearance of gratuities in the jurisdictional act and because of the success since the *Fort Berthold case* in 1930 in massing impregnable set-offs. That case represented the last reasonably large recovery by an Indian tribe. In the 24 cases since then only three claimants have recovered, only one of which recovered in the face of gratuities, and their total recovery was only slightly over one million, that is, $1,112,495.23.

This disposal of Indian cases is not an economy to the Government. The method of disposing of the claims has probably cost the Government more than would a system which operated more directly and efficiently and allowed a reasonable recovery on reasonable claims. It is probable that for the accounting alone in these 20 cases, the cost was nearly half the recovery in the three successful cases.

Furthermore, before 1920 when these Indian claims were relatively rare and were less of a legislative and administrative burden and expense, generous recoveries were allowed in almost all the cases. Only dissatisfaction and further expense can attend the present trend. While no argument is attempted in support of recovery, per se, it is obvious that if meritorious claims are to be almost automatically defeated, there is not much point in continuing the expensive farce of providing the claimants a day in court.

III. THE REMEDY OFFERED BY THE PROPOSED CLAIMS COMMISSION.

The Claims Commission is designed to improve the situation where it is weakest and most inefficient, that is, in the selection of claims which merit settlement, in the investigation of these claims, in the proper settlement of those claims which cannot appropriately be submitted to judicial action, and in the preparation of jurisdictional acts in such a way as to assure the most efficient and conclusive court action. But the Commission is designed also for a function even more important which, as has been demonstrated, cannot be achieved by the present handling of claims, that is, the final disposition of all Indian claims. If the Commission can dispose of Indian claims more efficiently and with finality and in 10 or 15 years instead of 100 or 150, it will result in a tremendous economy to the Government even though it may cost during the years of its existence more in direct outlay by the Government than the present method. Furthermore, if the Commission can dispose of Indian claims justly, it will result in a great gain and saving in the Government's relations with the Indians. How the Commission can effect these ends may be best described in outlining the functions of the Commission as they correspond to or supersede or relate to the existing system.

First, presentation of claims: Instead of a motley group of claims being presented to Congress from which a very few, chosen more or less haphazardly, emerge after an indefinite length of time with a jurisdictional act, there would be a commission directed and equipped to call in all outstanding Indian claims and to sift them separating the good from the bad.

(a) Provocation of ancient claims not to be feared. It may be argued that the fact that an agency is set up to hear all claims and that the Government encourages the bringing of all claims promptly and readily to this agency instead of discouraging claimants by strewing the path to the Court of Claims with obstacles will result in a large number of worthless claims being advanced and provoked by "ambulance-chasing" attorneys. Such a charge can be made against any agency or court which is reasonably available to everyone wishing to use it. Furthermore, we are not dealing with a class of people who are unprotected from designing attorneys. On the contrary all contracts with attorneys must be approved by the Secretary of the Interior (R. S. 2103) and in a matter of this kind where the attorney must work in cooperation with officials in the Interior Department through the necessity of obtaining information, it is unlikely that many ambulance chasers will get very far. But even if ancient and trumped-up claims are presented, it must be remembered that, as has been shown, they are even now frequently presented to Congress. With a commission set up especially to weed out such claims the Government will be better protected against them than at present when a preoccupied Congress is solicited and beguiled with political arguments. Furthermore, by section 4 of the bill the commission is authorized to receive claims for a period of only 5 years, with the important provision that all claims existing before such period not presented within such period shall be forever barred. This " statute of limitations " similar to the limitations imposed in jurisdictional acts, will operate to discourage somewhat the presentation of claims not already existing, since developing a claim often requires extensive research.

(*b*) As regards cessation of claims due to the limitation period: But the limitation period is important almost entirely because it is the key to the major purpose of the bill—the ending of the presentation of worthless claims and the final settlement of just Indian claims. While it is true that Congress has of course the power to extend this period by amendment or to give ear to particular claims later presented to it, it is very unlikely that Congress would so nullify the work of the Commission especially if its work is generally satisfactory. So far Congress has refused to reopen the question of claims to enrollment settled by the Dawes Commission or the work of the Court of Private Land Claims. Furthermore, by these provisions Congress indicates that not only will these claims be no longer acceptable before it, but that they will meet with no attention before other Federal agencies. There can be no complaint by a delinquent claimant of failure of notice of the limitation as by section 5 of the bill the Commission is required to send a written explanation of the provisions of the act to all potential claimants, i. e., all Indian tribes, bands or other communal groups.

While Congress may allow the Claims Commission to draw out its life unnecessarily, certain counter-arguments to this claim may be made. By section 11 of the bill the Commission is required to report annually to Congress of the progress of its work. This will act as a goad, as will the complaints to Congress of dissatisfied claimants, and the critical attitude of guardians of the public purse, like the Bureau of the Budget and the General Accounting Office.

But even if its work is prolonged unnecessarily, it will be speedier than the present system and will result in the ending of the work for all time as in the case of most other special commissions.

Second, investigation and sifting of claims: As indicated previously the Committees on Indian Affairs occasionally look rather thoroughly into the merits of claims presented for jurisdictional acts, but in doing so they must rely almost entirely upon the information given them by the claimant's attorney and upon the recommendation of the Indian Office; in any event, they cannot give close attention even to the majority of claims. After the act is passed, the objection is not so much to the failure of thoroughness as to the inefficiency, divided responsibility, expense and delay of the processes of investigation, as has been described.

Now, in regard to the improved method of investigation: In comparison with this slip-shod condition, the Commission will operate as an expert body equipped with personnel and given authority to make its own investigations of the facts from the Indians themselves and from the records in the Government offices, using Government assistants wherever the Government office will permit them to do so.

As a central unifying and directing agency it can bring system and order into the investigation of claims thus eliminating unnecessary work. It can develop standards, formulae for claims and patterns of research. For example, it can so arrange work that several related claims can be examined at once by agents in the field and by agents in the Government bureaus. The chief delay in the past at the point of investigating claims has been the fact that single sets of records must be examined and re-examined separately for different claims or different tribes. The Commission can so organize the work that a maximum amount of return can be secured from a single examination, and that photostatic copies of key records or other such devices to aid research will be used.

Eliminating unnecessary work: But more important than organizing work or personnel is the fact that the commission because of its difference in function from that of a court, can eliminate a tremendous amount of useless accounting which is now such an expensive burden. Thus, it is certainly unnecessary to prepare an elaborate report of all Government expenditures for a tribe to set off a claim which has no merit. Here is one signal economy of the Commission. It determines first the merits of the claim and then if necessary calls for set-offs. In some cases in order to determine the merits of a claim a report must be made from the Accounting Office as to whether payments have been made upon the claim, but such a report is a relatively simple and discrete matter and can be done separately without causing any later general accounting or duplication of effort. A great many claims can thus be disposed of without any, or with a minimum of work in the General Accounting Office. On this score then, the work of the General Accounting Office may be decreased rather than increased as has been feared. The overburdened Government offices may also be relieved by the fact that the Commission, empowered to employ assistants and do its own investigating, may take over a good deal of the work of the offices which can appropriately be transferred to it, as well as directing work by existing Government employees wherever such work is transferred to its supervision.

As to the cost and availability of personnel: On the question of expense, it is apparent that the bill contemplates the employment of a certain number of people not now on the Government's pay roll— the three commissioners and necessary assistants. If this be objected to on the ground of expense or of the difficulty of securing trained people, it must be remembered that the same problem would arise if the settlement of Indian claims were attempted by the enlargement of existing agencies without the creation of a commission. The objection to the probably initial expense of the Commission has already been discussed. On the subject of personnel, it seems unthinkable that there would not be a host of competent candidates for the offices of commissioners, among whom those with experience in Indian affairs would be preferred. Such experience is by no means rare. Many have been concerned with Indian affairs, as investigators, scholars in social sciences, advisers to and officials of the Government's administration of Indian affairs. But such experience is not necessarily essential. A mind competent to investigate and to judge will be competent to familiarize itself in hardly more than 6 months with the peculiar problems of the subject. Any enlargement of existing offices will require taking newcomers in at the bottom or at the top. In either case, training would be necessary. In 1925 the General Accounting Office was able to take on and train in a relatively short period about 80 new men to work on the great *Sioux case*. Their spokesman before the Senate subcommittee expressed no inability to use and train more people to expedite the work if necessary appropriations were made—hearings, at 13419. An assistant who has spent 6 months or a year in training and 9 years in serving the Commission would be a saving and not an expense to the Government. If the work is to be done and assistants employed to do it, it is better to have the work done in the most efficient manner possible than to patch up and enlarge an inefficient system.

Preference for commission over enlargement of existing agencies: The advantages of a special commission over the enlargement of existing agencies need not be far sought for. No one existing agency is in a position to undertake a comprehensive investigation of one claim, to say nothing of all claims. The most likely is the Department of the Interior, as it has the records upon which all land claims rely. But this Department is the appointed guardian of the Indians, their chief Government friend and counselor. For this reason, and the fact that many claims are based on alleged wrongs done by the Department, the Department has repeatedly sought to be relieved even of its duty of reporting to Congress on the merits of jurisdictional bills. Furthermore, many of the claims are based on financial dealings and some seek general accountings, and almost all information on these reposes in the General Accounting Office. The Department of the Interior cannot then determine the merits of those claims; and with both the Department and the General Accounting Office determining the merits of a great many claims, the present difficulties of conflict and confusion would only be aggravated rather than relieved. The General Accounting Office is unsuited for such determination, as it is the special guardian of the pocket of the defendant and is essentially an accounting and not a discretionary agency. The only possible existing agencies are thus too narrowly specialized, and each represents one of the parties to the claim. An impartial, expert, broadly discretionary commission is imperative.

Third, determination of facts: The determination of the facts revealed by the investigation is a chief function of the commission and the one which makes the commission at once so necessary and so valuable. While an impartial body is necessary to investigate the facts, this alone is hardly worth-while unless the commission is empowered to take the next step which is the logical culmination of its research and make positive findings of fact. Furthermore, such findings are necessary if the commission is expected and empowered to draw conclusions as to the merits of the claims.

As to finality of determinations: But to make the work of the commission really worth-while the highest degree of finality consistent with the legislative and judicial processes to follow should attach to its determinations. The claimant is provided with an expert forum, with sufficient notices and ample opportunities to be heard (secs. 5, and 8). After such procedure determinations of fact are normally accorded finality so long as the finding is based upon evidence, as in the case of the great number of administrative tribunals set up in the last 25 years, to find facts. (*Dahlstrom Metallic Door Co.* v. *Industrial Board*, 284 U. S. at 594 (1932). See *Crowell* v. *Benson*, 285 U. S. 22, at 47–50 (1932) ; II Wigmore, Evidence (2d Edition 1923) secs. 1347, 1355.) However, this commission differs from the normal fact-finding commission in that its determinations take the form of reports to Congress and only Congress can take final action upon the findings or submit the matter to the Court of Claims when it considers that legal questions may require judicial determination. For this reason, the normal rule of law which excludes judicial review of administrative findings would not apply to the findings of the commission unless Congress so stated in submitting the claim to the Court of Claims. It is, of course, impossible to bind Congress on this subject in advance. But a statement of the policy and intent of Congress as to the respect to be accorded the determinations of the commission can and should be made in this bill to advise claimants and the commission as well as future Indian Affairs Committees. Therefore it is provided (sec. 3) that in all proceedings brought in the Court of Claims all determinations of fact by the commission shall be accorded prima facie weight. The determinations are made of prima facie rather than of conclusive weight in order to permit the Court of Claims to review the evidence before the commission and to weigh new evidence in those cases where the antagonist of the determinations can bring forward sufficient proof to combat the presumption of correctness which shields the commission's actions and which will ordinarily be sufficient protection against attack. In other words, the findings of the commission will be prima facie evidence of the facts, which, in terms of judicial action, means that the court can accept these facts as proved and rest its decisions upon them in all cases except where an opposing party may have successfully borne the burden of disproof. Thus the court is authorized to accept the findings as sufficient; but it is not precluded from examining into any phase of the actions of the commission when it finds compelling reason to do so. (*Meeker & Co.* v. *Lehigh Valley R. R. Co.*, 236 U. S. 412 (1915) ; *Chicago B. & O. R. R. Co.* v. *Jones*, 149 Illinois 361, 37 N. E. 247 (1894).) A similar provision is found in section 16 (2) of the Transportation Act of 1920 (49 U. S. C. A., sec. 16 (2)), which makes the finding of the Interstate Commerce Commission prima facie evidence of the facts in trials to enforce a reparation order. The many cases in the Supreme Court discussing the provision have analyzed it as having the effect set forth above. (*Pennsylvania R. R. Co.* v. *Weber*, 257 U. S. at 85; *Atchison, Topeka & Santa Fe Railway Co.* v. *Spiller*, 252 U. S. at 117; *Mills* v. *Lehigh Valley Railroad Co.*, 238 U. S. at 473; *Meeker & Company* v. *Lehigh Valley Railroad Co.*, *supra; Southern Railway Co.* v. *St. Louis Hay Co.*, 214 U. S. at 297.)

It is contemplated, however, that the vast majority of determinations by the commission will never reach the court but will be the basis of action by Congress in the direct settlement of claims. In these situations, if the work of the commission has been satisfactory, it is highly probable that the determinations will be readily accepted by Congress as conclusive.

Fourth, ascertainment of merits. Appropriateness of a commission to ascertain the merits of claims: On the basis of the facts which it has found, the commission will perform its most serviceable function—making findings as to the merits of each claim. This function implies a certain amount of discretion but does not necessarily require any legal or other special skill but simply a certain amount of common sense plus a familiarity with the situations which give rise to Indian claims generally and with the background of the particular claim. At this point again an expert commission is particularly valuable. While Indian claims are now sometimes examined, individually, the connection between one claim and another, their common background and the general policy of the Government in relation to all the Indians over a number of years obviously was not and could not have been seen in the past. Placing a claim in such perspective will assure a far greater accuracy in the determination of its merits than does the present individual inspection. Because Congress and the Indian Affairs Committees are unable to weed out the worthless claims, it is necessary, as interested persons agree, to have an agency to perform this duty. Obviously it should be the same agency which is familiar with all the facts, not just part of them, and one which holds an impartial position.

Previous recognition of the desirability of a commission to sift claims: The proposal to remedy the defects in the present system of handling claims by the use of a Claims Commission with the functions as outlined in H. R. 7837 is not entirely new. The Meriam investigators came to the conclusion that the solution of the problem lay in the establishment of a special commission to study the claims not yet submitted by Congress to the Court of Claims and to make recommendations to be submitted to Congress through the Secretary of the Interior with a draft of a suitable bill transferring meritorious claims to the Court of Claims. Meriam, The Problem of Indian Administration, 1928, at 48. Commissioner Rhoads, testifying before the subcommittee of the Senate Committee on Indian Affairs, argued the need for a commission preferably separate from the Interior Department to separate meritorious claims from those without merit and possibly to make findings of fact and to render judgment accordingly. In this connection, he said: " Our most pressing need at this time is some sort of machinery to act as a sifter or separator so that meritorious claims may be separated from those without merit." Survey of Conditions of the Indians in the United States, part 25, hearings, January 22, 1930, at 13409. On this occasion Senator Wheeler agreed that such a commission would be a time-saving device. Hearing, at 13411. Back in 1913 Commissioner Meritt had come to the same conclusion that the only satisfactory solution was a commission to investigate claims, to sort them and to prepare reports upon which Congress could dispose of the cases for all time. See Hearings before the subcommittee of the House Committee on Indian Affairs on the appropriation bill for 1914, at 99.

Fifth, recommendations to Congress: On the basis of the facts and the merits of the claims the Commission will make recommendations to Congress as to the appropriate disposition to be made of the claim. If the claim has no merit; for example, if it had been paid or if a previous settlement had been made of it and release given and there were no compelling reason for reopening the settlement, the Commission would recommend the denial of further consideration of such claim. It is believed that a great many claims can be disposed of in this way, thus obviating the present necessity of prolonged petitioning of Congress and possibly of extended and useless research in the Government departments.

Final settlement of most claims by Congress: Of the claims that have merit, probably the vast majority will be recommended for settlement and will be settled by Congress in the manner recommended by the Commission. It is contemplated that the Commission will recommend for settlement all meritorious claims where the parties do not insist upon going to the Court of Claims for determination of a disputed question of law. If the Commission does competent work such insistence should be rare. Furthermore, as has been previously discussed, certain claims can be given relief only by the political branch of the Government no matter how many questions of law are involved, particularly those which seek relief for fraud, mistake, or duress in the making of treaties. Therefore all claimants on those points must content themselves with the relief that Congress acting upon the advice of the Claims Commission will give them.

Total recovery not great. This may result, of course, in the payment of claims which otherwise might not be paid until the claimant single-handed could get relief from Congress, but it will result in the avoidance of the lost time in going to the Court of Claims and in the removal of all pleas for relief and in the redress of all claims which Congress has recognized to be just. Furthermore, the total recovery will probably not exceed $100,000,000 at the very most, which allows for many times the amounts recovered in the past litigated cases. There is, of course, no way of estimating the number of claims which will be submitted not the amount of money which will be claimed. But it is well known that the face value of claims has no relation to the final amount awarded, especially after the application of generous set-offs; for example, although the claims heard by the Court of Claims between 1893 and 1928, inclusive, demanded several billions of dollars, the total recovery was but $18,515,670.

Where the claim is settled by Congress or where it has been sent to the Court of Claims under an adequately prepared jurisdictional act and is decided in favor of the claimants, it need not be feared that a drain upon the Treasury resources will result. The payment of the claims need not involve for the time being more than a matter of bookkeeping on the Treasury records. But as many tribes are frequently in dire need of funds for productive uses it may be that these funds can be made available to them when appropriations for their benefit cannot be made.

Conclusion: In conclusion it may be said that the result of the establishment of an Indian Claims Commission and its performance of the designated work will be the relief of Congress from the continuous onslaught of bills for jurisdictional acts, the competent advising of Congress on the final disposition of all Indian claims and the quieting of all these claims within a comparatively brief period and a very decided improvement in the effectiveness of Government work among the Indians.

Mr. Chairman, that concludes my prepared statement.

The Chairman. Are there any questions?

Mr. Dimond. Mr. Chairman, I wonder if it would be convenient for Mr. Poole to furnish a mimeographed copy of that?

The Chairman. Yes; he has said that he will do that. Are there any other questions? The time is growing short and the committee will soon have to conclude. We will now hear from Mr. Blair, the Assistant Attorney General.

STATEMENT OF HON. HARRY W. BLAIR, ASSISTANT ATTORNEY GENERAL, DEPARTMENT OF JUSTICE

Mr. Blair. Mr. Chairman and gentlemen, I doubt if there is anything that I can add to this presentation by Mr. Poole. However, may I call attention to a small matter? It is in connection with what was said a while ago about an Indian being a member of the commission.

It might be that this committee would deem it advisable in order to get a strictly impartial commission that there be some provision as to political profession. In regard to the three commissioners, it is frequently provided that no more than two should belong to the same political party. That might help some. What is desired by all of us is to get a constant and an impartial commission to handle it and eliminate all question of doubt, and that, I think, would be helpful.

In regard to the bill there is another feature of it that I would also like to call attention to. It is a matter that I am not prepared to give a written statement on because I have not had an opportunity to look into that question.

On page 4 of the bill it provides that this commission may request of the General Accounting Office such information as in the judgment of the commission is required for the determination of set-offs. Then the bill further provides that the determination of the facts by the commission shall be prima facie. I am not clear in my mind as yet as to whether that would mean that if the commission made a report as to facts that on the basis of the facts, a transcript of which would be transferred to the Court of Claims, that it would not be possible on the basis of those same facts to hold that their conclusion as to the ultimate facts were wrong. In other words, what is the meaning of the prima facie findings? That is the only point about it that if I may have the privilege I would like to write something on the order of what was presented here this morning.

The Chairman. We will be glad, indeed, to have you present a brief on that point, and it may be inserted in the record at the end of your statement.

Mr. Blair. Thank you. We are very much in favor of the bill. We think the principle of the bill is right, that it will speed up the settlement of these claims. There are a great many claims by Indian tribes that have no real basis, but the Indian tribes having those claims are entitled to their day in court before this commission and the tribe should present those claims and be heard and if at that time the commission turns them down they would have the feeling that they had been given an opportunity to be heard and I think that would have a good influence, a splendid influence in the relations between the Government and many of those tribes.

There are many other claims that are just from a standpoint of fair and square dealings which while not being based upon any legal grounds cannot be heard by the Court of Claims under the jurisdictional acts that have been passed. A great many of those claims are entitled to consideration; they are entitled to remuneration. A great many of those claims should be paid as a matter of honest man-to-man square dealings and this bill will enable that to be done by the Commission making a report and Congress making a direct appropriation. That is all I care to say.

Mr. DIMOND. Mr. Chairman.

The CHAIRMAN. Mr. Dimond.

Mr. DIMOND. I was wondering as a legal question or a matter of law whether all claims would be embraced within general equitable principles. I have not noticed in the bill that those things may be based on general equitable principles.

Mr. BLAIR. Yes, sir.

Mr. DIMOND. All right. There is one other thing, if I may ask the question, and either one of you gentlemen may answer. I am not quite clear as to whether the hearings and all of these things would be done within a period of 5 years.

Mr. POOLE. It is not necessary, they may be presented.

Mr. DIMOND. Thank you.

Mr. BLAIR. I am not clear as to the bill in that regard. The bill provides that the commissioners shall be appointed for the life of the commission but nowhere in here is the life of the commission fixed. If the commission were appointed tomorrow I very much doubt if under the bill you could say for how long it was appointed.

Miss WESTWOOD. Mr. Chairman, in section 11 of the bill it is provided in line 22 " the commission shall cease to exist on the fulfillment of its duties under this act; or, in any event unless extended by act of Congress, on the expiration of 10 years after the formal organization of the commission. When the commission shall cease to exist, all its books, documents, letters, official records, and all papers shall be transferred to the Indian Office."

Mr. BLAIR. That makes it clear.

The CHAIRMAN. Mr. Blair, you said you would like to make a written statement for inclusion in the hearing.

Mr. BLAIR. Yes, sir.

The CHAIRMAN. And you would like to have it included in the hearing. What does the committee desire?

Mr. BURDICK. I would like to have a copy of it.

The CHAIRMAN. Congressman Burdick asks that by unanimous consent the Department of Justice be permitted to submit a written statement to be included in the hearing. Is there any objection? As there is no objection, it will be so ordered.

(The statement of Mr. Blair is as follows.)

MAY 28, 1935.

Hon. WILL ROGERS,
  Chairman Committee on Indian Affairs,
    House of Representatives, Washington, D. C.

MY DEAR MR. ROGERS: As I stated to the committee, I am very heartily in favor of the establishment of a commission along the lines provided in the Indian Claims Commission bills (H. R. 7837; S. 2731).

It is the view of the Department that the second paragraph of section 3, which provides that in all proceedings brought pursuant to the bill in the Court of Claims, all determinations of fact by the commission shall be accorded prima facie weight. It is felt that it is important that the parties to a litigation in the Court of Claims should have the opportunity to argue before the court the question as to whether or not the findings of the commission are justified by the weight of the evidence submitted, and to propose other findings on the basis of the evidence taken before the commission. There is some doubt whether, under the pending measure, the Court of Claims would have the authority to review the commission's findings of facts in the absence of additional evidence submitted to the court to contravert the findings made by the commission.

Accordingly, it is suggested that the second paragraph of section 3 of the bill be modified to read as follows:

"In all proceedings brought pursuant hereto in the Court of Claims, all determinations of fact made by the commission shall be admissible in evidence, but may be reviewed by the court either on the basis of the evidence taken before the commission or on additional evidence, or both."

Respectfully,
                            HARRY W. BLAIR,
                          Assistant Attorney General.

The CHAIRMAN. I understand that Mr. Poole would like to make a brief statement.

Mr. POOLE. I would like to make an observation before concluding and that is this:

In considering the number of commissioners that should be appointed to this commission there was no unanimity or feeling on the part of those who prepared the bill. We arrived rather arbitrarily at the figure 3, but many of us thought that probably a larger commission would serve the purposes of this legislation more adequately.

Commissioner COLLIER. My personal thought was that five ought to serve.

Mr. DIMOND. If you have a large number on the commission there may be some difficulty in regard to it.

The CHAIRMAN. The original bill provided for five commissioners.

Commissioner COLLIER. There is the thought that in case of a large commission the commission might split up into groups.

The CHAIRMAN. The committee can amend the bill, of course, if it feels that the commission should be made larger.

Mr. BURDICK. I would like to make this statement: After hearing counsel on this bill it is my idea right now, I think that there should be a commission of 5, 2 associate commissioners to be Indians and 2 of anyone else, and those 4 to select the final commissioner and then when you have an Indian claim and turn it down it will be turned down and that will be the end of it, and if you do not have the Indians on it, they will come back to the next Congress.

The CHAIRMAN. Is there anything further that anyone wishes to ask?

Mr. POOLE. Mr. Chairman, as a clarifying amendment we would like to suggest that in section 2 where we have outlined the type of claims that could be presented to the Commission in that particular section, the four different classes that are provided for we would like to insert an amendment in line 19 immediately after the word " all ", and the amendment to consist of the insertion of the words " claims founded upon the Constitution, laws, or treaties of the United States and all."

It might be implied from the language that now exists that such claims could be received, but in order to remove any doubt I think those words should be placed in the bill.

The CHAIRMAN. The Chair would like to make this request, that at the beginning of the hearing the bill should be inserted in the record.

Mr. DIMOND. I ask unanimous consent that that be done.

The CHAIRMAN. If there is no objection, it is so ordered.

Is there any other comment concerning the bill? If not, a motion to adjourn will be in order.

I wish at this time to thank the representatives of the Interior and the Justice Departments for the statements that they have presented today. If there is nothing else to come before before the committee, we will now stand adjourned.

(Thereupon, at 12 m., the committee adjourned to meet at the call of the chairman.)

INDIAN CLAIMS COMMISSION ACT

HEARINGS

BEFORE THE

COMMITTEE ON INDIAN AFFAIRS
UNITED STATES SENATE

SEVENTY-FOURTH CONGRESS

FIRST SESSION

ON

S. 2731

A BILL TO CREATE AN INDIAN CLAIMS COMMISSION,
TO PROVIDE FOR THE POWERS, DUTIES, AND
FUNCTIONS THEREOF, AND FOR
OTHER PURPOSES

JUNE 10 AND 17, 1935

Printed for the use of the Committee on Indian Affairs

UNITED STATES
GOVERNMENT PRINTING OFFICE
WASHINGTON : 1935

19C9

II

Library of Congress Cataloging in Publication Data

United States. Congress. Senate. Committee on Indian
Affairs.
    Indian Claims Commission act.

    Issued with the reprint of the 1935 ed. of United States.
Congress. House. Committee on Indian Affairs. Indian Claims
Commission. New York [1976].
    Reprint of the 1935 ed. published by U. S. Govt. Print. Off.,
Washington.
    1. United States. Indian Claims Commission.   2. Indians
of North America—Claims.   I. Title.
KF27.I45 1935b   343'.73'025   76-11750
ISBN 0-404-11982-4

AMS PRESS, INC.
NEW YORK, N. Y.

INDIAN CLAIMS COMMISSION ACT

MONDAY, JUNE 10, 1935

United States Senate,
Committee on Indian Affairs,
Washington, D. C.

The committee met, pursuant to call, at 10:30 a. m., in room 424, Senate Office Building, Senator Elmer Thomas (chairman) presiding. Also present: Hon. William Zimmerman, Jr., Assistant Commissioner of Indian Affairs; Rufus G. Poole, Assistant Solicitor, Interior Department; Harry Blair, Assistant Attorney General; and S. M. Dodd, Chief Finance Officer, Indian Service.

The Chairman. The bill that is set for hearing this morning is the Indian Claims Commission bill, S. 2731. It was, on request, introduced by myself. Mr. Zimmerman, by whom was this bill drawn?

Mr. Zimmerman. In the Solicitor's Office in the Interior Department. It was drawn after consultation with the Department of Justice.

The Chairman. Who is present that is prepared to explain to the committee the necessity for the bill, and just what this bill does?

Mr. Zimmerman. Mr. Poole, representing the Solicitor of the Interior Department, is here; and Mr. Harry Blair, Assistant Attorney General, is also here to speak for the Department of Justice. They are both more familiar with the details that am I.

The Chairman. At this point I will insert in the record a copy of the bill, S. 2731, and also a copy of the letter from the Secretary of the Interior.

(The bill is as follows:)

[S. 2731, 74th Cong., 1st sess.]

A BILL To create an Indian Claims Commission, to provide for the powers, duties. and functions thereof, and for other purposes

Be it enacted by the Senate and House of Representatives of the United States of America in Congress assembled, That a Commission be, and hereby is, created and established to be known as the "Indian Claims Commission", which shall be composed of a Chief Commissioner and two Associate Commissioners, who shall be appointed by the President, by. and with the advice and consent of the Senate. The Commissioners shall continue in office during the existence of the Commission or until resignation or removal by the President only for inefficiency, neglect of duty, or malfeasance in office. Vacancies in the Commission shall be filled by the President in the same manner as original appointments. No vacancy shall interrupt the functioning of the Commission, nor impair the right of the remaining Commissioners to exercise all of its powers and to perform all its duties. The Commissioners shall not engage in any other business, vocation, or employment during their term of office. Each of the Commissioners shall receive an annual salary of $10,000 payable in the same manner as the salaries of judges of the courts of the United States.

1

Sec. 2. It shall be the duty of the Commission to investigate all claims against the United States of any Indian tribe, band, or other communal group of American Indians residing within the territorial limits of the United States of Alaska, to ascertain and determine all of the facts relating thereto and all questions of mixed law and fact as may be incidental to such determination, and, on the basis of the facts found by it, to ascertain and determine the merits of all such claims and to make findings with reference thereto. Such claims shall include all those whether sounding in contract or tort or otherwise with respect to which the claimant would have been entitled to redress in any court of the United States if the United States were subject to suit; and all claims of whatsoever nature on account of any breach of duty committed by any officer or agent while purporting to act in the name or on behalf of the United States; and all further claims under all treaties heretofore negotiated between the claimant and the United States but not formally ratified or executed by all of the parties thereto; and those claims of whatsoever nature which would arise on a basis of fair and honorable dealings unaffected by rules of law, and those which would result if the treaties, contracts, and agreements between the claimant and the United States were revised on the ground of fraud, duress, or mutual or unilateral mistake whether of law or fact. Any such claim now pending in the Court of Claims, and any such claim previously referred to Congress to the Court of Claims and not yet filed in such court may be transferred, together with all the documents and certified copies of all the records relating thereto, by the complainant to the Commission at any time within the period provided for presentation of claims to the Commission, and all further proceedings with respect thereto shall be had under the provisions of this Act regardless of the terms of any act giving jurisdiction of such claim to the Court of Claims. No claim shall be excluded because of the provisions of any other statute; nor because it has already been presented to the Congress; nor on the ground that it has become barred under any rule of law or equity, or by reason of any treaty or statute; nor on the ground of a prior adjudication with respect thereto in any judicial, administrative, or other proceeding between the same parties: *Provided, however,* That the Commission, when ascertaining the merits of any claim, shall take into consideration, and may inquire into, all previous adjudications or settlements of such claim and all payments made by the United States on its account. In any case wherein the Commission determines that a claim has merit under the provisions of this Act, the General Accounting Office and the Indian Office upon request of the Commission shall furnish such information as in the judgment of the Commission is required for the determination of set-offs.

Sec. 3. The Commission shall make a detailed report to the Congress of its findings of the facts of each claim, the conclusions reached as to the merits of such claim and the reasons therefor, together with an appropriate recommendation for action or nonaction by that body. If any claim shall be ascertained to be without merit in law or in fact, the Commission shall so report. If any claim shall be found to rest on some legal, equitable, or sound moral obligation, the recommendation shall be for a direct appropriation by the Congress in a specific amount, or other adequate relief, or for the passage of an Act giving jurisdiction of such claim to the Court of Claims.

In all proceedings brought pursuant hereto in the Court of Claims all determinations of fact by the Commission shall be accorded prima facie weight.

Sec. 4. The Commission shall be authorized to receive claims for a period of five years after the approval of this Act and no claim existing before such period not presented within such period may thereafter be submitted to any Federal court or administrative agency for consideration or action, nor will such claim be entertained by Congress.

Any claim within the provisions of this Act may be presented to the Commission by any member or members of an Indian tribe, band, or other communal group, as representative of all such members, regardless of the present status of such members as allottees, citizens or unrestricted Indians; but wherever any tribal organization exists, recognized by the Secretary of the Interior as having authority to represent such tribe, band, or group, such organization shall be accorded the exclusive privilege of representing such Indians, unless fraud, collusion, or laches on the part of such organization be shown to the satisfaction of the Commission.

Sec. 5. Immediately after its formation, the Commission shall send a written explanation of the provisions of this Act to the recognized head of each Indian tribe and band, and to any other communal groups of Indians existing as a distinct entity, and shall request that a detailed statement of all claims be sent to the Commission, together with the names of aged or invalid Indians from whom immediate depositions should be taken and a summary of their proposed testimony.

SEC. 6. The recognized representatives of each such tribe, band, or other communal group of Indians may retain to represent its interests in the presentation of claims before the Commission an attorney-at-law, whose employment and the terms thereof shall be subject to the provisions of sections 2103, 2104, 2105, and 2106 of the Revised Statutes, and whose practice before the Commission shall be governed by rules and regulations hereby authorized to be formulated by the Commission. The Attorney General or his assistants shall represent the interests of the United States in connection with all matters pertaining to this Act.

SEC. 7. The Commission shall make a complete and thorough search for all evidence affecting such claims, utilizing all documents and records in the possession of the Court of Claims and the several Government bureaus and offices. The Commission or any of its members or authorized agents may hold hearings, examine witnesses, and take depositions in any place in the United States, and any of the commissioners may sign and issue subpenas for the appearance of witnesses and the production of documents from any place in the United States or Alaska at any designated place of hearing. In case of disobedience to a subpena, the Commission may obtain an order from any court of the United States requiring obedience to that subpena; and any failure to obey such order shall be punished by such court as a contempt thereof. Witnesses subpenaed to testify before the Commission, witnesses whose depositions are taken pursuant to this Act, and the officers or persons taking the same, shall severally be entitled to the same fees and mileage as are paid for like services in the courts of the United States.

SEC. 8. The Commission shall give notice and an opportunity for a hearing to the interested parties before making any final determination upon any claim. A full written record shall be kept of all hearings and proceedings of the Commission and shall be open to inspection by the attorneys concerned. Whenever a final determination is reached by the Commission upon any claim, notice thereof shall be given to the tribe, band, or group concerned. Within twenty days thereafter written objections thereto may be filed with the Commission by any interested party. If such objections are not accepted by the Commission, they shall be recorded as a part of the report on the claim presented to the Congress.

SEC. 9. The Commission may adopt all such rules for its own procedure, for the organization of its work, and for the effectuation of the purposes of this Act as it may deem appropriate. The Commission may employ and fix the terms of employment of such experts, field investigators, and professional and clerical assistants as may be necessary to fulfill duties which cannot be properly performed by persons already engaged in the Government service. At the Commission's request, the General Accounting Office, the Land Office, and the Bureau of Indian Affairs may transfer or temporarily assign to the Commission such of their employees as are specially qualified to assist the Commission in the performance of any of its duties under this Act.

SEC. 10. All necessary expenses of the Commission, including all reasonable traveling expenses incurred by the Commissioners, or under their orders, upon official business in any place outside the city of Washington, and including necessary expenses for suitable rooms and equipment for the principal office of the Commission in the city of Washington and for the performance of duty outside the city of Washington, shall be allowed and paid on the presentation of itemized vouchers therefor approved by the Chief Commissioner.

SEC. 11. Annual reports shall be submitted by the Commission to Congress showing the progress of its work. The Commission shall cease to exist on the fulfillment of its duties under this Act; or, in any event unless extended by Act of Congress, on the expiration of ten years after the formal organization of the Commission. When the Commission shall cease to exist, all its books, documents, letters, official records, and other papers shall be transferred to the Indian Office.

SEC. 12. There is authorized to be appropriated for the purpose of carrying out the provisions of this Act such sums as the Congress may from time to time determine.

SEC. 13. This Act may be cited as the " Indian Claims Commission Act."

(The report of the Secretary of the Interior follows:)

INTERIOR DEPARTMENT,
Washington, June 5, 1935.

Hon. ELMER THOMAS,
Chairman Committee on Indian Affairs,
United States Senate.

MY DEAR MR. CHAIRMAN: Reference is made to your request of May 2 for a report on S. 2731, a bill to create an Indian Claims Commission to investigate and determine the facts and the merits of all existing claims by Indian tribes against the United States and to report its findings with appropriate recommendations to Congress.

The proposed commission, to be composed of three commissioners appointed by the President with the advice and consent of the Senate, is authorized to make a thorough search for all evidence on the facts involved in such claims, but may make determinations only after notice and hearing to all the interested parties. It is contemplated that the Commission shall received claims for a period of 5 years and that its work shall be completed within 10 years after its creation. It may report its recommendation to Congress as its determinations are made, and annual reports to Congress of the progress of its work are required.

The bill does not itself provide for the adjudication of any Indian claim. Its purpose is to expedite the handling of such claims, to provide Congress with competent, impartial advice on the disposition of the numerous requests by Indian tribes for the passage of jurisdictional acts or the allowance of appropriations, and to relieve the Court of Claims of the burden of highly complicated and necessarily prolonged fact determination.

Congress is now endlessly confronted with the challenge (*a*) to enact direct settlements with Indian tribes, and (*b*) to enact jurisdictional bills which more or less predetermine the ultimate settlement, in both cases without any adequate data upon which to reach a decision. Nor can this data be accumulated through legislative hearings in Washington. The immediate and, if necessary, sufficient justification of the pending bill lies in the above fact and in the way the bill would change that fact.

As a result of inadequate data, the jurisdictional acts, among other peculiarities, often are inconsistent with one another, sometimes in the direction of leniency, and sometimes in the opposite direction, and in few or none of them are the authorizations and limitations based upon the particular and local history of the tribe and of its relations with the Government.

At present, after long preliminary negotiation and lobbying, eventuating in a jurisdictional act, a petition is filed in the Court of Claims, and the General Accounting Office goes through all records of expenditures, accumulating as certain or possible set-offs the detailed record of all the gratuitous expenditures for or in behalf of each tribe. The Indian Office, simultaneously or subsequently, prepares a lengthy history and discussion of the case. While the General Accounting Office is working on one case many others are waiting their turn, because much of the data is contained only in a single, unduplicated series of badly worn-out records.

After many years spent in preparation the Government and the tribe go into combat before the Court of Claims under a jurisdictional act which usually is believed and admitted by all the parties to be inequitable, and which does not and should not have the character of an act for final settlement. Largely because of the unsatisfactory character of the acts, recovery in the Court of Claims by Indian tribes has become very infrequent, with resulting justifiable dissatisfaction by the tribes and their return to Congress for further redress.

The total operation is greatly influenced by elements of sheer accidents, such as the possession by Indians of the wherewithal to hire attorneys for the initial lobbying of their case.

The above unsatisfactory state of affairs would be completely changed through the work of the Commission under the pending bill. The Commission would dispose of real and alleged claims, tribe by tribe. Its recommendations, whether for direct settlement or for jurisdictional acts, would be merely recommendations so far as Congress and the Budget were concerned, but its findings of fact would be a permanent accomplishment. The Commission would be empowered and expected to take into account the particular historical circumstances of each tribe—its treaties and its land occupancy and its subsequent fate at the hands of the Government—and its present needs. In the ascertainment of set-offs the Commission would prepare for submission to Congress a total of possible set-offs such as in the Commission's judgment may be fair in the light of the particular circumstances. In contrast to the present system set-offs other than direct payments upon the claim need not be searched for except in the case of claims already determined to have merit, thus saving effort and expense. Furthermore, in asecertaining set-offs the Commission would be in a position to prevent inequality of treatment by applying standards for the direction of research. Through photostating some of the records in the General Accounting Office, the Commission would be able to dispose simultaneously of the set-off questions affecting numerous tribes. The Commission would draw into its total picture the information in the possession of the Office of Indian Affairs—information which ordinarily, at present, is not put together until after a jurisdictional act, with all its fatalities, has become law.

Based upon the findings of fact and the recommendations of the Commission, there undoubtedly will be many cases where Congress and the tribes can readily agree upon a direct final settlement, thus making unnecessary any litigation in the Court of Claims or the Supreme Court of the United States.

Where such direct settlement may prove to be not feasible because of unsettled legal questions, the claim may be submitted to the Court of Claims under an act framed on the basis of the research of the Commission to present adequately all the issues requiring determination. As the findings of the Commission are made prima facie evidence of the facts of the claim, further investigation of such facts is in most cases rendered unnecessary.

There will be no need of paying to private attorneys amounts which have aggregated millions and which, before the final settlement is achieved under the now existing arrangement, would total tens of millions.

A somewhat increased cost to the Government (i. e., simply the expenses of the Commission itself) will be balanced by a permanent reduction of costs in the Indian Office, the General Accounting Office, the Department of Justice, and the courts. And, finally, it will be possible for the Indians, Congress, and the country to know with a clear conscience that at least the facts have been ascertained and that the merits of the cases are set down in an adequate manner. It is believed that just, final settlement would follow as a matter of course.

I recommend enactment of Senate bill 2731.

The Assistant Director of the Bureau of the Budget has advised that this bill " would not be in conflict with the financial program of the President if section 3 were amended in accordance with the recommendation contained in the attached copy of the Attorney General's letter to me of May 24, 1935, and if section 9 were amended to provide that the employees of the Commission shall be subject to the provisions of the Classification Act of 1923, as amended."

To comply with the suggestion of the Assistant Director of the Budget, the words " subject to the provisions of the Classification Act of 1923, as amended ", set off by commas, could be inserted on page 7, line 24, after the word " employ."

The amendment suggested by the Attorney General would be, on page 4, line 25, to strike out the words " accorded prima facie weight " and to insert " admissible in evidence, but may be reviewed by the Court either on the basis of evidence taken before the Commission or on additional evidence or both."

Sincerely yours,

HAROLD L. ICKES, *Secretary of the Interior.*

Report of the committee on S. 2731 follows:

The Committee on Indian Affairs, to whom was referred the bill (S. 2731) to create an Indian Claims Commission, to provide for the powers, duties, and functions thereof, and for other purposes, having considered the same, report thereon with a recommendation that it do pass with the following amendments:

On page 2, line 19, after the word " all " insert the words " Claims arising under the Constitution, laws, or treaties of the United States."

On page 3, line 14, change the word " Complainant " to read " Complainants."

On page 3, line 16, after the word " and " insert the following words: in connection with claims so transferred."

On page 3, line 18, strike out the word " terms " and insert in lieu thereof the word " provisions " and after the word " any " insert the words " other law or of any " and change the word " claim " to read " claims."

On page 3, line 19, change the period to a colon and insert the following:

"*Provided,* That in cases now pending in the Court of Claims the transfer thereof to the Commission shall be made upon motion of the attorney of record for claimant in each case with the approval of the Secretary of the Interior and such attorney or attorneys shall proceed under his or their approved existing contract according to its terms."

On page 4, line 15, after the period, insert the following words:

" Such report shall show how each Commissioner voted upon such claims."

On page 6, line 6, after the word " attorney " insert a comma and the words " or attorneys."

On page 6, line 20, after the comma, insert the words " or Alaska."

On page 7, line 24, after the word " employ " insert the following words:

" Subject to the provisions of the Classification Act of 1923, as amended."

This bill proposes to create an Indian Claims Commission to investigate and to determine the facts and the merits of all existing claims of Indian tribes against the United States and to report its findings with appropriate recommendations to Congress.

The Commission would be composed of three commissioners, appointed by the President with the advice and consent of the Senate, and would be equipped with the usual powers of a fact-finding commission to hold hearings and to examine witnesses. The Commission is directed to "make a complete and thorough search for all evidence" affecting claims upon its own initiative through investigations in the field and in Government records, utilizing in doing so, insofar as possible, Government employees now qualified in the work.

The interests of the Indian claimants in the investigations and determinations of the Commission are amply protected by the provisions of the bill requiring notice to all possible claimants, and notice and opportunity for hearing to all interested parties before making findings on any claim, and authorizing representation by attorneys.

Upon the completion of its investigations the Commission will make formal findings of fact and recommendations to Congress for action or nonaction upon the claims by Congress. If the claim has no merit, Congress will be so informed and may disregard such claim thereafter. However, where the claim has merit, the Commission will recommend either a direct settlement, or in those few cases where judicial action may be unavoidable, jurisdictional act giving adequate jurisdiction of such claim to the Court of Claims. Before the Court of Claims the findings of fact made by the Commission are to be accorded prima facie weight.

It is provided that all existing claims must be presented to the Commission within 5 years and that the work of the Commission will end after 10 years from the date of approval of the act. Annual reports of the progress of its work are required to be presented to Congress.

The outstanding benefits which would follow the establishment of such a commission may be summarized as follows:

1. The proposed method of handling Indian claims will expedite necessary work and will eliminate a great volume of unnecessary work since it will be free of the present divided responsibility between the Department of the Interior, Department of Justice, and General Accounting Office, and since the Commission can direct and standardize research, discard at the outset worthless claims, and avoid duplication of research by handling related claims simultaneously.

2. The Commission will be prepared to determine claims in a more competent manner than that afforded by the present system. Instead of hasty, political decisions by Congress upon individual jurisdictional bills, and haphazard and partisan preparation of the claim for trial, the Commission, as an impartial expert body, will assume the burden of investigation and the accurate advising of Congress in an authoritative and conclusive manner.

3. A commission, acting as adviser to Congress, offers the only way in which claims founded upon political wrongs, mainly those claims which seek revision of, or compensation for, inequitable treaties, can be settled. The Court of Claims repeatedly dismisses such claims for lack of jurisdiction, placing at no avail the prolonged effort required to reach that court.

4. From the foregoing it is evident that great expense will be saved the Government and the Indians. The present cumbersome and inconclusive method, estimated to require a century to reach completion, means increasing direct and tangible costs to the Government and prohibitive expense or exorbitant outlay of tribal funds to the tribes.

5. Finally, just determination and settlement of just claims will improve the morale of the Indians and the effectiveness of the Government service among them.

Representatives of the Department of Justice, Department of the Interior, attorneys representing Indian tribes, and representatives of Indian welfare organizations were present at hearings which were held on this bill, who suggested various amendments to the bill, some of which were adopted by the committee and are recommended in this report. Said representatives of the Departments and others representing various interests manifested their approval generally of this proposed legislation.

The CHAIRMAN. Will you state your name to the committee, please?

Mr. POOLE. Rufus G. Poole.

The CHAIRMAN. What position do you occupy?

Mr. POOLE. Assistant Solicitor for the Interior Department.

The CHAIRMAN. We have before the committee, S. 2731, a bill to create an Indian Claims Commission, to provide for the powers, duties, and functions thereof, and for other purposes. Were you instrumental in the preparation of this bill?

Mr. POOLE. I was.

The CHAIRMAN. Will you please state to the committee the reasons making necessary some further legislation, then follow that up by explaining the terms of this bill to the committee, as briefly as you can?

Mr. POOLE. Mr. Chairman, this is a very complicated problem and it has a considerable historical background that I think should be considered as a justification for this legislation.

I have prepared here a statement 32 pages in length that deals with the question rather completely. I have that available for each member of the committee if so desired, or I can read it and treat with it more briefly at the present time.

The CHAIRMAN. Inasmuch as this is a very important bill and it is proposed to change the processes through which the Indians must go to present their claims for justice at the hands of the Government, in all probability it would be well to go through your statement.

Mr. POOLE. This bill would, if enacted, establish an Indian Claims Commission with the purpose of achieving a rapid, final, and just disposition of all outstanding Indian claims against the Government. The Commission, composed of three commissioners appointed by the President with the advice and consent of the Senate, would perform four major functions: (1) The investigation of existing Indians claims; (2) the determination of all facts relating thereto; (3) the ascertainment of the merits of the claims; and (4) the report to Congress of the facts and the merits of the claims with specific recommendations for the settlement of meritorious claims or for a jurisdictional act to transfer meritorious claims which involve disputed legal questions to the Court of Claims.

The reasons which make this bill important may be discussed under three major headings: (1) The necessity for prompt and just disposition of Indian claims; (2) the inadequacy of the present method of disposing of Indian claims; and (3) the remedy offered by the proposed Claims Commission.

First I will deal with the necessity for prompt and just disposition of Indian claims:

Investigators of Indian affairs and successive commissioners have insisted that the Government's administration of Indian affairs is in a large measure ineffective and futile so long as the tribes have claims against the Government which they believe to be just. The Meriam study of the problem of Indian administration (1928) expressly finds that [reading]:

The existence of these claims is a serious impediment to progress. The Indians look forward to getting vast sums from these claims; thus their economic future is uncertain. They will hardly knuckle down to work while they still hope the Government will pay what they believe is due them (p. 19). The disturbing influence of outside agitators seeking personal emoluments and the conviction in the Indian mind that justice is denied, renders extremely difficult any cooperation between the Government and its Indian wards (p. 805).

At the hearings held 5 years ago by the subcommittee of the Senate Committee on Indian Affairs for the purpose of investigating the problem of the slowness of the prosecution of Indian claims, the settlement of these claims was accepted by the Senators and by the Indian Commissioners as a fundamental need. See Survey of Conditions of the Indians in the United States, part 25, hearings, hereinafter referred to simply as hearings, Seventy-second Congress, first session, January 22, 1930, at 13409, et sequentia. See also the testimony of Commissioner Meritt at the hearings before the subcommittee of the House Committee on Indian Affairs on the appropriation bill for 1914, at page 99; and to the same effect the annual report of the Secretary of the Interior, 1934, at page 83.

Furthermore, the present method of handling those claims which have received attention only aggravates the situation, since, as will be demonstrated in some detail, it postpones their settlement an almost indefinite time, and in the meanwhile wastes the substance of the claimants and puts the Government to heavy expense, and results mainly in disappointment and unjustified defeat.

I come now to the second point, the inadequacy of the present method of disposing of Indian claims:

No solution of the problem is promised by the present system which not only is highly inefficient in functioning but fails to accomplish its task of settling Indian claims and settling them justly. The system was investigated by the subcommittee of the Senate Committee on Indian Affairs in 1930 and many of its deficiencies were then disclosed. Drawing upon the facts presented to that subcommittee and upon information available from other Government records and other studies of the situation, an analysis can be made of each step in the present process of settling a claim, revealing the defects which make the whole process slow, expensive, and fruitless.

By way of summary it may be said at this point that the process is slow because it normally takes several years and much lobbying to secure a jurisdictional act, and because, on the average, 10 years then pass before the claim comes to trial. It is also expensive for these reasons plus the fact that much of the labor is unnecessary. And it can be termed fruitless because 21 of the 24 cases decided since 1930 were dismissed, and of these 21 at least five and probably more were dismissed because an otherwise valid recovery was submerged by a preposterous system of set-offs. The slowness of the system can be indicated by the fact that about 70 of the petitiones filed in the Court of Claims which had been pending for many years at the time of the subcommittee investigation in 1930 are still pending. It is true that the disposition of cases which was just over one a year before 1930 has increased to just over five a year since then; one reason for this increase is that many of the extensive and complicated accounting reports which had required 3 to 5 years of the General Accounting Office's time and probably cost in some instances $25,000 a piece were completed fairly recently. The slowness of the system may also be indicated by the fact that the 24 cases which have been decided since 1930 have required on the average 8½ years from the time Cogress assented to their suits until their decision. Today there are 98 petitions pending in the Court of Claims.

The number of claims which still seek settlement, besides these 98 now pending, including those that come back to Congress after unsatisfactory treatment and those which have not yet been presented to Congress, cannot be estimated. Suffice it to point out that since the first session of the Sixty-ninth Congress 96 bills have been presented which Congress did not act upon. At the present rate of progress there would appear to be more than one century ahead of troublesome Indian claims.

Better than by summary statistics, the defects of the present system can be demonstrated by an analysis of the functioning of its several processes.

The first step is getting the claim before Congress. Here some tribes are baffled, not sure how to make definite and press their claims. See the statements and questions of Indians about the claims of their tribes made to subcommittee of the Senate Indian Affairs Committee taking testimony in various western States (hearings at pp. 13609–13670) and others are the victims of self-seeking attorneys. Even normally, however, the success which a tribe has in getting its case before Congress depends on such irrelevant matters to the merits of its case as its wherewithal to employ the necessary investigators and attorneys, and its sophistication in doing so.

Perhaps the most disheartening of all the various labors in pushing a claim is the work of securing a jurisdictional act.

In less harassed congressional sessions than the present a great many of these jurisdictional bills flood in, all presenting peculiar and complicated fact situations which in only a very few situations can a committee adequately study. In 1930 there were 49 such bills before the Congress (see letter of Senator Thomas to the Attorney General, hearings, p. 13526); there were at least 25 presented to the Seventy-third Congress. The present Congress is burdened with 20 original and 9 amendatory bills. But these bills are persistent plaintiffs and return session after session, despite disregard, defeat, and veto, and regardless of whether they are meritorious or not. For example, since the first session of the Sixty-ninth Congress the Oregon Indians have presented their claims 9 times, and the Colville and Okanogan Indians 6 times.

The few bills which are finally passed are those fortunate enough to secure correct political backing, often regardless of the merits of the claim. Admittedly political considerations dominate in a situation which should be governed solely by judicial considerations.

Much depends upon the standing in Congress of the sponsors of the bill, upon the composition of the Committees on Indian Affairs, and upon the attitude of the administration (Meriam report, op. cit., supra, pp. 805–806).

The attitude of the administration is one of the variable and political elements, not only because of the possibility of a veto but because of the fact that each jurisdictional bill is sent to the Interior Department for a report. The bill which repeatedly comes before Congress may receive sometimes a favorable and sometimes an unfavorable report; for example, in the case of the jurisdictional bills for the California Indians, within 6 years they received twice favorable and twice unfavorable reports. (See Meriam, op. cit., supra, p. 806.)

A somewhat similar fate befell the bills for the Iowa Indians in spite of a fairly careful study and endorsement of the claim by the House Indian Committee only the second time the bill was presented. (See S. Rept. No. 303, 64th Cong., 1st sess., Mar. 25, 1916, incorporating H. Rept. No. 1398, 62d Cong., 3d sess.) The Indian Office and the Interior Department have many times protested against this reference of jurisdictional bills to them for report, contending that as they are obligated to be the special guardian and chief friend of the Indian, and as many of the claims are founded on alleged administrative errors in the more or less remote past, it is frequently inappropriate and difficult to make such decision. (See Hearings, at 13410.)

The result is that before a jurisdictional act is finally secured many years must frequently be consumed in agitation, propaganda, and lobbying (Meriam, op. cit. supra, p. 806).

The Indian claimants must meet the expense of attorneys, representatives, witnesses, delays, and defeats, and often, of trying their case twice, once before the committee and once before the Court of Claims. As supporter of the Indians the Government must ultimately meet this same expense as well as the expense of the continuous delay and harassment of Congress. Obviously this cost to the Government of this blind repetitious process is enormous.

Further waste attendant upon the system is the passage of stillborn acts, acts which can bring the claimants little or no benefit. This grows out of the fact that Congress is an inappropriate body to pass upon Indian claims without having responsible, impartial advice.

In one case, that of the Turtle Mountain Chippewa, the jurisdictional bill had been presented five times to Congress. Finally in 1933 it was passed, only to be vetoed; and was repassed in 1934, again only to be vetoed. It is now again before Congress in another form. The veto rested on the fact that the claim in effect demands the reformation of a treaty—a thing the Court of Claims cannot and will not do (*Sisseton and Wahpeton Indians* v. *United States*, 58 C. Cl., 302 (1923); affirmed *Sisseton and Wahpeton Indians* v. *United States*, 277 U. S. 424 (1928)). Despite this fundamental objection the claim will continually be pressed before Congress and because it appeals to the sense of justice, may finally be given a jurisdictional act only to be dismissed from the Court of Claims 10 or 20 years later after arduous work by the General Accounting Office, the Indian Office, the Department of Justice, and the attorneys for the Indians.

Congress does not appear to learn that a great many claims cannot be settled by the Court of Claims but only by political action, in spite of the fact that all the many claims which sought relief from fraud, duress, or mistake of fact, and which have been sent to the Court of Claims were dismissed for want of jurisdiction. The court repeatedly said, first, that the stereotype language of the jurisdictional act regularly employed, " all claims arising under any treaty ", did not permit consideration of claims attacking rather than relying on the treaty; and, secondly, that in any event the reformation of treaties was a political function which Congress could not constitutionally place upon the judicial branch. (*Otoe and Missouria Indians* v. *United States*, 52 C. Cl., 424 (1917), (claim based on inadequate consideration for treaty cession) ; (*Sisseton and Wahpeton Indians* v. *United States*, 58 C. Cl., 302 (1923), (claim based on mistake and misrepresentation as to the acreage ceded by treaty) ; *Creek Nation* v. *United States*, 63 C. Cl., 270 (1927), (claim for value of land ceded without consideration and because of duress) ; *Osage Tribe of Indians* v. *United States*, 66 C. Cl., 64 (1928), (claim for proceeds of sale of land because of inability to understand the words of the treaty).)

The doctrine has firm roots in Supreme Court decisions. (*United States* v. *Old Settlers*, 140 U. S. 427 (1893) ; *United States* v. *Choctaw, etc., Nations*, 179 U. S. 494 (1900) ; *Sisseton and Wahpeton Indians* v. *United States*, 277 U. S. 424 (1928). It must be noted that if the treaties in these cases had been contracts between ordinary individuals, in most of them, if complete evidence had been allowed, an equity court would have allowed reformation, so that the claims in these cases can be considered " merely moral " only because they relate to treaties. In the *Osage case*, supra, even a law court might well have doubted whether there were any contract as there obviously occurred no " meeting of the minds." Moreover, the Court of Claims is inclined to consider itself as helpless to reform agreements between the United States and the Indians as treaties. (See *Klamath and Moadoc, etc., Indians* v. *United States*, No. E. 346 (Apr. 8, 1935), p. 12; but compare *Iowa Tribe of Indians* v. *United States*, 68 Ct. of Cl., 585 (1920), (recovery of additional compensation based upon an oral agreement).) In this Iowa case the court was influenced by the unusually broad and explicit language of the jurisdictional act.

Although in a great many cases the language of the jurisdictional act is decisive of the claim, the language is often deficient not only in the way previously discussed, but sometimes because it is restricted to specific claims under specific treaties (cf. Ute Indian Act of Mar. 3, 1909, 35 Stat. 788), or too broad (cf. Sioux Indian Act of June 3, 1920, 41 Stat. 738, all " amounts, if any, due said tribe from the United States   *   *   * "), or does not cover the type of claim which the tribe has (cf. *Choctaw and Chickasaw Nation* v. *United States*, 75 Ct. of Cl., 494). The reason is that the acts do not reflect the history of the tribe and cannot do so as long as they must lack the study which should attend them.

The greatest injustice done by the jurisdictional acts is, however, the utterly inconsistent and irrational provisions for set-off. Some acts will provide simply for set-off of payments made upon the claim, others will allow also for set-off of counterclaims, as in the act founding the Creek claims, May 24, 1924 (43 Stat. 139), which are usually the unpaid parts of reimbursable agreements, but the most devastating of all is the increasingly frequent allowance in acts of set-off of gratuities. Congress has shown a strange partiality in this provision. It has usually avoided placing it in the jurisdictional acts for the Five Civilized Tribes, and placed it in others.

The set-off of gratuities means that all money ever spent by the United States in any way for the benefit of the tribe may be deducted by the court from the recovery won by the tribe. Because the matter can be settled only piecemeal in court, neither the Department of Justice nor the General Accounting Office has any definite or consistent standard as to what is for the benefit of the tribe (Hearings, p. 13418). As a result none of the parties can gage the strength of his case. When the General Accounting Office reports a gratuity set-off so large that recovery appears to be out of the question, the lawyer for the claimants does not end the case, as he does not know how many of the items included in the report the Department of Justice and the Court of Claims will reject as not appropriately deducted as gratuities; or he may seek an amendment of the jurisdictional act to strike out set-off of gratuities. This was the dilemma that confronted the lawyer in the Klamath general accounting cases, no. E–350, reported out of the General Accounting Office in 1928, and apparently not yet decided (Pt. 25, Senate hearings, at pp. 13480, 13481).

The shocking inconsistency in the various holdings of the Court of Claims as to what may be deducted from the recovery won by the tribe as a gratuity may be illustrated by the following citations. Sometimes the Court of Claims allows the Government set-off for educating the tribe's children in nonreservation Indian schools (*The Blackfeet, Blood, etc., Tribes* v. *The United States*, no. E–427, Apr. 8, 1935), and sometimes it does not (*Fort Berthold Indians* v. *United States*, 71 C. Cls., 308). More fatal to recovery is the allowance of a set-off of all the money the Government has spent in the administration of Government agencies, as for superintendents, interpreters, teachers, Indian police, agency buildings, and so forth (*The Duwamish, Lummi, etc., Tribes* v. *The United States*, no. F–275, June 4, 1934), on the ground that these things are benefits to the Indians. But in another case the court said it should exclude such items recognizing that the maintenance of a Government agency is simply the performance of a governmental function and an obligation incurred by the United States in developing the reservation policy; and furthermore that such expenditures are common expenditures for all tribes (*The Assiniboine Tribe* v. *The United States, no.* J–31, Apr. 10, 1933). Sometimes the court has realized that this argument should exclude set-offs for money expended for education and civilzation, but normally the court allows deduction even for this (*The Duwamish, Lummi, etc., Tribes* v. *The United States, supra; The Crow Nation* v. *The United States, supra*). Sometimes the court does not bother to analyze and reject erroneous deductions in the accounting prepared by the General Accounting Office saying that the total set-off is so large that the Indian tribe has no hope of recovery anyway (*The Crow Nation* v. *The United States, supra*).

The result is as follows:

The deduction for money which obviously the Government would have spent and has spent for all tribes not only is grossly unfair to the tribes with just claims against the Government for wrongs done them by the Government, but it has resulted in the fact that since 1929 in every case but two where the jurisdictional act allowed set-off of gratuities and where a recovery has been won in the court the petition has been dismissed because the recovery was exceeded by the set-offs.

Could anything be so wasteful or so futile in fulfilling its purpose of quieting Indian claims as the continuous dismissal of just and proven claims either because the court has no jurisdiction of them or because the recovery is blotted out by the Government? It is obvious that if this policy is continued it will be more and more hopeless for the Indians to sue the Government except on very extravagant claims, for the amount of the Government expenditures in carrying out its Indian policies is increasing enormously daily.

The result of inadequate jurisdiction acts is that after an act is passed, the claimant returns for amendments. Probably more than half the acts passed have been subjected to amendments. Far more wasteful than this result is, however, the lack of finality which must result when a just claim has not been given justice in the Court of Claims, either because of rules of law or otherwise. Congress is constantly being petitioned for new acts for the benefit of claims which have been decided in the Court of Claims (see, for example, the Otoe and Missouria bill, S. 2560, and the Stockbridge and Munsee bill, H. R. 5230, now before Congress and each introduced twice before), and occasionally Congress grants the request (see *Delaware Tribe* v. *United States*, 72 C. Cls., 525 (1931)), and the whole wasteful process of preparation begins again.

I next take up the preparation of the case:

The unsatisfactory features of the present system do not end with the defective jurisdictional acts. The practice is for the Department of Justice upon receipt of the tribe's petition after its filing in the Court of Claims to send copies of the petition with a form letter to the Department of the Interior and to the General Accounting Office. Since the Department of Justice is naturally uninformed of the facts of the claim, the form letter can contain no analysis of the petition and no instructions as to the information desired; it simply requests all the information which the Interior Department or the Office may have on the subject. (Hearings, at 13522, 13577.) Inevitably a very great deal of time, even many years, is wasted in the accumulation by the Department and especially the General Accounting Office of a mass of material which later is found to be unnecessary and irrelevant. (Hearings, at 13494, 13499.)

Furthermore, many of the cases arise from the action of the Government in dealing with land which has no relation to the books of account and do not require accounting. Thus, in the Osage case, there was nothing but a question of law and it was decided on that basis (66 Court of Claims, 69), but the case had to be delayed for about 4 or 5 years for reports costing, as was estimated, about $25,000 or $30,000. (Hearings, at 13522.)

This was the situation in 1930 and it may have improved since then, but certain inherent defects cannot be removed or improved under the present system. These defects lie in the fact that every petition no matter how patently or latently worthless on its facts, if it is not dismissed on a point of law on demurrer, causes years of search not only into the facts, but at the same time into all the possible set-offs and defenses.

This means that every claim, particularly where other set-offs are allowed than simply payments upon the claim, is held up for the 2 to 10 years which is necessary to do a general accounting of all financial matters between the Government and the tribe sometimes as far back as 1789, although such set-offs might never be needed because the claim could be dismissed as worthless on the facts. This defect is due to the fact that because of the nature of a judicial trial both sides must be ready on all points at the same time. The inappropriateness of trying to settle Indian claims indiscriminately by trial before the Court of Claims is apparent from this one fact alone.

I will next take up the trial of the case:

There are no complaints about the administrative efficiency of the Court of Claims. Indian claims when ready for trial receive prompt attention. Informed and interested persons have always denied that the notorious delay in the disposal of Indian claims was due to crowded dockets or congestion in the court itself. (Hearings, at 13413.) For this reason the solution of the Indian claims problem proposed in 1930 in H. R. 7963, namely the creation of a separate Court of Indian Claims, was officially rejected by the Department of the Interior and the Department of Justice and instead amendments to the bill or alternative proposals were suggested to set up a claim-sifting commission on the order of that proposed in the bill that is now under consideration. Congressional Record, June 27, 1930, at 11901 et seq.; letter of Attorney General Mitchell to the Director of the Bureau of the Budget, March 11, 1930.

Failure of recovery: The extravagant effort and expense that the Government and the Indians have put into the disposition of Indian claims have brought little good to the Indians especially in recent years. Of those claims which were really meritorious and deserved attention and which worked their way to the Court of Claims, some were dismissed because the court denied jurisdiction of the substance of their claim, some were dismissed because the language of the jurisdictional act was unfortunately drawn, and some were dismissed because the set-offs wiped out the recovery. This last reason has played a more and more prominent role because of the increasing frequency of the appearance of gratuities in the jurisdictional act and because of the success since the Fort Berthold case in 1930 in massing impregnable set-offs. The case represented the last reasonably large recovery by an Indian tribe. In the 24 cases since then only three claimants have recovered, only one of which recovered in the face of gratuities, and their total recovery was only slightly over one million, that is, $1,112,495.23.

This disposal of Indian cases is not an economy to the Government. The method of disposing of the claims has probably cost the Government more than would a system which operated more directly and efficiently and allowed a reasonable recovery on reasonable claims. It is probable that for the accounting alone in these 20 cases, the cost was nearly half the recovery in the three successful cases.

Furthermore, before 1920 when these Indian claims were relatively rare and were less of a legislative and administrative burden and expense, generous recoveries were allowed in almost all the cases. Only dissatisfaction and further expense can attend the present trend. While no argument is attempted in support of recovery, per se, it is obvious that if meritorious claims are to be almost automatically defeated, there is not much point in continuing the expensive farce of providing the claimants a day in court.

I will next take up the remedy offered by the proposed claims commission:

The claims commission is designed to improve the situation where it is weakest and most inefficient, that is, in the selection of claims which merit settlement, in the investigation of these claims, in the proper settlement of those claims which cannot appropriately be submitted to judicial action, and in the preparation of jurisdictional acts in such a way as to assure the most efficient and conclusive court action. But the commission is designed also for a function even more important, which, as has been demonstrated, cannot be achieved by the present handling of claims, that is, the final disposition of all Indian claims. If the commission can dispose of Indian claims more efficiently and with finality and in 10 or 15 years instead of 100 or 150, it will result in a tremendous economy to the Government even though it may cost during the years of the existence more in direct outlay by the Government than the present method. Furthermore, if the commission can dispose of Indian claims justly, it will result in a great gain and saving in the Government's relations with the Indians. How the commission can effect these ends may be best described in outlining the functions of the commission as they correspond to or supersede or relate to the existing system:

Instead of a motley group of claims being presented to Congress from which a very few, chosen more or less haphazardly, emerge after an indefinite length of time with a jurisdictional act, there would be a commission directed and equipped to call in all outstanding Indian claims and to sift them separating the good from the bad.

It may be argued that the fact that an agency is set up to hear all claims and that the Government encourages the bringing of all claims promptly and readily to this agency instead of discouraging claimants by strewing the path to the Court of Claims with obstacles will result in a large number of worthless claims being advanced and provoked by " ambulance chasing " attorneys. Such a charge can be made against any agency or court which is reasonably available to everyone wishing to use it. Furthermore, we are not dealing with a class of people who are unprotected from designing attorneys. On the contrary, all contracts with attorneys must be approved by the Secretary of the Interior, and in a matter of this kind, where the attorney must work in cooperation with officials in the Interior Department through the necessity of obtaining information, it is unlikely that many ambulance chasers will get very far. But even if ancient and trumped-up claims are presented, it must be remembered that, as has been shown, they are even now frequently presented to Congress. With a commission set up especially to weed out such claims the Government will be better protected against them than at present, when a preoccupied Congress is solicited and beguiled with political arguments. Furthermore, by section 4 of the bill the commission is authorized to receive claims for a period of only 5 years, with the important provision that all claims existing before such period not presented within such period shall be forever barred. This "statute of limitations" similar to the limitations imposed in jurisdictional acts will operate to discourage somewhat the presentation of claims, not already existing, since developing a claim often requires extensive research.

But the limitation period is important almost entirely because it is the key to the major purpose of the bill—the ending of the presentation of worthless claims and the final settlement of just Indian claims. While it is true that Congress has, of course, the power to extend this period by amendment or to give ear to particular claims later presented to it, it is very unlikely that Congress would so nullify the work of the commission, especially if its work was generally satisfactory. So far Congress has refused to reopen the question of claims to enrollment settled by the Dawes Commission or the work of the Court of Private Land Claims. Furthermore, by these provisions Congress indicates that not only will these claims be no longer acceptable before it but that they will meet with no attention before other Federal agencies. There can be no complaint by a delinquent claimant of failure of notice of the limitation, as by section 5 of the bill the commission is required to send a written explanation of the provisions of the act to all potential claimants; that is, all Indian tribes, bands, or other communal groups.

While Congress may allow the claims commission to draw out its life unnecessarily, certain counterarguments to this claim may be made. By section 11 of the bill the commission is required to report annually to Congress of the progress of its work. This will act as a goad, as will the complaints to Congress of dissatisfied claimants, and the critical attitude of guardians of the public purse, like the Bureau of the Budget and the General Accounting Office. But even if its work is prolonged unnecessarily, it will be speedier than the present system and will result in the ending of the work for all time as in the case of most other special commissions.

The investigation and sifting of claims:

As indicated previously the Committees on Indian Affairs occasionally look rather thoroughly into the merits of claims presented for jurisdictional acts, but in doing so they must rely almost entirely upon the information given them by the claimant's attorney and upon the recommendation of the Indian Office; in any event, they cannot give close attention even to the majority of claims. After the act is passed, the objection is not so much to the failure of thoroughness as to the inefficiency, divided responsibility, expense, and delay of the processes of investigation as has been described.

In comparison with this slipshod condition, the Commission will operate as an expert body equipped with personnel and given authority to make its own investigations of the facts from the Indians themselves and from the records in the Government offices, using Government assistants wherever the Government office will permit them to do so. As a central unifying and directing agency it can bring system and order into the investigation of claims thus eliminating unnecessary work. It can develop standards, formulas for claims, and patterns of research. For example, it can so arrange work that several related claims can be examined at once by agents in the field and by agents in the Government bureaus. The chief delay in the past at the point of investigating claims has been the fact that single sets of records must be examined and reexamined separately for different claims or different tribes. The Commission can so organize the work that a maximum amount of return can, be secured from a single examination, and that photostatic copies of key records or other such devices to aid research will be used.

But more important than organizing work or personnel is the fact that the Commission, because of its difference in function from that of a court, can eliminate a tremendous amount of useless accounting which is now such an expensive burden. Thus, it is certainly unnecessary to prepare an elaborate report of all Government expenditures for a tribe to set off a claim which has no merit. Here is one single economy of the Commission which is very important. It determines first the merits of the claim, and then if necessary calls for set-offs. In some cases, in order to determine the merits of a claim a report must be made from the Accounting Office as to whether payments have been made upon the claim, but such a report is a relatively simple and discrete matter and can be done separately without causing any later general accounting or duplication of effort. A great many claims can thus be disposed of without any, or with a minimum of work in the General Accounting Office. On this score then, the work of the General Accounting Office may be decreased rather than increased as has been feared. The overburdened Government offices may also be relieved by the fact that the Commission, empowered to employ assistants and do its own investigating, may take over a good deal of the work of the offices which can appropriately be transferred to it, as well as directing work by existing Government employees wherever such work is transferred to its supervision.

On the question of expense, it is apparent that the bill contemplates the employment of a certain number of people not now on the Government pay roll—the three commissioners and necessary assistants. If this be objected to on the ground of expense or of the difficulty of securing trained people, it must be remembered that the same problem would arise if the settlement of Indian claims were attempted by the enlargement of existing agencies without the creation of a commission. The objection to the probable initial expense of the Commission has already been discussed. On the subject of personnel, it seems unthinkable that there would not be a host of competent candidates for the offices of commissioners, among whom those with experience in Indian affairs would be preferred. Such experience is by no means rare. Many have been concerned with Indian affairs, as investigators, scholars in social sciences, advisers to and officials of the Government's administration of Indian affairs for years. But such experience is not necessarily essential. A mind competent to investigate and to judge will be competent to familiarize itself in hardly more than 6 months with the peculiar problems of the subject. Any enlargement of existing offices will require taking newcomers in at the bottom or at the top. In either case training would be necessary. In 1925 the General Accounting Office was able to take on and train in a relatively short period about 80 new men to work on the great *Sioux case.* Their spokesman before the Senate subcommittee expressed no inability to use and train more people to expedite the work if necessary appropriations were made. Hearings, at 13419. An assistant who has spent 6 months or a year in training and 9 years in serving the Commission would be a saving and not an expense to the Government. If the work is to be done and assistants employed to do it, it is better to have the work done in the most efficient manner possible than to patch up and enlarge an inefficient system.

The advantages of a special commission over the enlargement of existing agencies need not be far sought for. No one existing agency is in a position to undertake a comprehensive investigation of one claim, to say nothing of all claims. The most likely is the Department of the Interior, as it has the records upon which all land claims rely. But this Department is the appointed guardian of the Indians, their chief Government friend and counselor. For this reason, and the fact that many claims are based on alleged wrongs done by the Department, the Department has repeatedly sought to be relieved of its duty of reporting to Congress on the merits of jurisdictional bills. Furthermore, many of the claims are based on financial dealings and some seek general accountings, and almost all information on these reposes in the General Accounting Office. The Department of the Interior cannot then determine the merits of those claims; and with both the Department of the Interior and the General Accounting Office determining the merits of a great many claims, the present difficulties of conflict and confusion would only be aggravated rather than relieved. The General Accounting Office is unsuited for such determination, it is believed, as it is the special guardian of the pocket of the defendant and is essentially an accounting and not a discretionary or judicial agency. The only possible existing agencies are thus too narrowly specialized and each represents one of the parties to the claim. An impartial, expert, broadly discretionary commission is imperative.

The determination of the facts revealed by the investigation is a chief function of the Commission and the one which makes the Commission at once so necessary and so valuable. While an impartial body is necessary to investigate the facts, this alone is hardly worth while unless the Commission is empowered to take the next step which is the logical culmination of its research and make positive findings of fact. Furthermore, such findings are necessary if the Commission is expected and empowered to draw conclusions as to the merits of the claims.

I will next deal with the finality of determinations:

But to make the work of the Commission really worth while the highest degree of finality consistent with the legislative and judicial processes to follow should attach to its determinations. The claimant is provided with an expert forum, with sufficient notices and ample opportunities to be heard, by sections 5 and 8. After such procedure determinations of fact are normally accorded finality so long as the finding is based upon evidence as in the case of the great number of administrative tribunals set up in the last 25 years to find facts. (*Dahlstrom Metallic Door Co. v. Industrial Board*, 284 U. S. 594 (1932). See *Crowell* v. *Benson*, 285 U. S. 22, 47–50 (1932); II Wigmore, Evidence (2d Ed. 1923) secs. 1347, 1355.) However, this Commission differs from the normal fact-finding commission in that its determinations take the form of reports to Congress and only Congress can take final action upon the findings or submit the matter to the Court of Claims when it considers that legal questions may require judicial determination.

For this reason, the normal rule of law which excludes judicial review of administrative findings would not apply to the findings of the Commission unless Congress so stated in submitting the claim to the Court of Claims. It is, of course, impossible to bind Congress on this subject in advance. But a statement of the policy and intent of Congress as to the respect to be accorded the determinations of the Commission can and should be made in this bill to advise claimants and the Commission as well as future Indian Affairs Committees. Therefore it is provided by section 3 that in all proceedings brought in the Court of Claims all determinations of fact by the Commission shall be accorded prima facie weight.

I should state at this point that there was some question raised about the advisability of that provision when the bill was under preparation. It was introduced in that form, but since that time the Attorney General and the Bureau of the Budget have advised that that be modified, and submitted an amendment to us which is incorporated in our report on the bill. We—some of us in the Interior Department, at least—regard that as rather vital, and I have prepared a short brief on that particular point, which I would like to submit for your consideration and information. However, our official recommendation on the bill embodies the amendment which the Department of Justice offered, which I pointed out before.

The determinations are made of prima facie rather than of conclusive weight in order to permit the Court of Claims to review the evidence before the Commission and to weigh new evidence in those cases where the antagonist of the determinations can bring forward sufficient proof to combat the presumption of correctness which shields the Commission's actions and which will ordinarily be sufficient protection against attack.

In other words, the findings of the Commission will be prima facie evidence of the facts which, in terms of judicial action, means that the court can accept these facts as proved and rest its decision upon them in all cases except where an opposing party may have successfully borne the burden of disproof. Thus the court is authorized to accept the findings as sufficient; but it is not precluded from examining into any phase of the actions of the Commission when it finds compelling reason to do so. *Meeker & Co.* v. *Lehigh Valley R. R. Co.* (236 U. S. 412 (1915)); *Chicago, B. & Q. R. R. Co.* v. *Jones* (149 Ill. 361, 37 N. E. 247 (1894)). A similar provision is found in section 16 (2) of the Transportation Act of 1920 (49 U. S. C. A., section 16 (2)), which makes the finding of the Interstate Commerce Commission prima facie evidence of the facts in trials to enforce a reparation order. The many cases in the Supreme Court discussing the provision have analyzed it as having the effect set forth above. *Pennsylvania R. R. Co.* v. *Weber* (257 U. S. 85); *Atchison, T. & S. F. R. Co.* v. *Spiller* (253 U. S. 117); *Mills* v. *Lehigh Valley R. Co.* (238 U. S. 473); *Meeker & Co.* v. *Lehigh Valley R. R. Co.*, supra; *Southern Railway Co.* v. *St. Louis Hay Co.* (214 U. S. 297).

It is contemplated, however, that the vast majority of determinations by the Commission will never reach the Court of Claims but will be the basis of action by Congress in the direct settlement of claims. In these situations, if the work of the Commission has been satisfactory, it is highly probable that the determinations will be readily accepted by Congress as conclusive.

On the basis of the facts which it has found, the Commission will perform its most serviceable function—making findings as to the merits of each claim. This function implies a certain amount of discretion but does not necessarily require any legal or other special skill but simply a certain amount of common sense plus a familiarity with the situations which give rise to Indian claims generally and with the background of the particular claim. At this point again an expert commission is particularly valuable. While Indian claims are now sometimes examined, individually, the connection between one claim and another, their common background and the general policy of the Government in relation to all the Indians over a number of years obviously was not and could not have been seen in the past. Placing a claim in such perspective will assure a far greater accuracy in the determination of its merits than does the present individual inspection. Because Congress and the Indian Affairs Committees are unable to weed out worthless claims, it is necessary, as interested persons agree, to have an agency to perform this duty. Obviously it should be the same agency which is familiar with all the facts, not just part of them, and one which holds an impartial position.

The proposal to remedy the defects in the present system of handling claims by the use of a claims commission with the functions as outlined in this legislation is not entirely new. The Meriam investigators came to the conclusion that the solution of the problem lay in the establishment of a special commission to study the claims not yet submitted by Congress to the Court of Claims and to make recommendations to be submitted to Congress through the Secretary of the Interior with a draft of a suitable bill transferring meritorious claims to the Court of Claims (Meriam, The Problem of Indian Administration, 1928, at 48). Commissioner Rhoads, testifying before the subcommittee of the Senate Committee on Indian Affairs, argued the need for a commission preferably separate from the Interior Department to separate meritorious claims from those without merit and possibly to make findings of fact and to render judgment accordingly. In this connection he said:

Our most pressing need at this time is some sort of machinery to act as a sifter or separator so that meritorious claims may be separated from those without merit (Survey of Conditions of the Indians in the United States, part 25, hearings, Jan. 22, 1930, at 13409).

On this occasion Senator Wheeler agreed that such a commission would be a time-saving device, and so stated in the hearings, at page 13411. Back in 1913 Commissioner Meritt had come to the same conclusion—that the only satisfactory solution was a commission to investigate claims, to sort them, and to prepare reports upon which Congress could dispose of the cases for all time. (See hearings before the subcommittee of the House Committee on Indian Affairs on the appropriation bill for 1914, at 99.)

On the basis of the facts and the merits of the claim, the Commission will make recommendations to Congress as to the appropriate disposition to be made of the claim. If the claim has no merit—for example, if it had been paid or if a previous settlement had been made of it and release given and there were no compelling reason for reopening the settlement—the Commission would then recommend the denial of further consideration of such claims. It is believed that a great many claims can be disposed of in this way, thus obviating the present necessity of prolonged petitioning of Congress and possibly of extended and useless research in the Government departments.

Of the claims that have merit, probably the vast majority will be recommended for settlement and will be settled by Congress in the manner that I have stated before. It is contemplated that the Commission will recommend for settlement all meritorious claims where the parties do not insist upon going to the Court of Claims for determination of a disputed question of law. If the Commission does competent work, such insistence, I think, will be rare. Furthermore, as has been previously discussed, certain claims can be given relief only by the political branch of the Government, no matter how many questions of law are involved, particularly those which seek relief for fraud, mistake, or duress in the making of treaties. Therefore, all claimants on those points must content themselves with the relief that Congress, acting upon the advice of the Claims Commission, will give them.

This may result, of course, in the payment of claims which otherwise might not be paid until the claimant, single-handed, could get relief from Congress, but it will result in the avoidance of the lost time in going to the Court of Claims and in the removal of all pleas for relief and in the redress of all claims which Congress has recognized to be just.

Furthermore, the total recovery will probably not exceed $100,000,-000 at the very most, which allows for many times the amounts recovered in the past litigated cases. There is, of course, no way of estimating the number of claims which will be submitted nor the amount of money which will be claimed. But it is well known that the face value of claims has no relation to the final amount awarded, especially after the application of generous set-offs; for example, although the claims heard by the Court of Claims between 1893 and 1928, inclusive, demanded several billions of dollars, the total recovery was but $18,515,670.

Where the claim is settled by Congress or where it has been sent to the Court of Claims under an adequately prepared jurisdictional act and is decided in favor of the claimants, it need not be feared that a drain upon the Treasury resources will result. The payment of the claims need not involve for the time being more than a matter of bookkeeping on the Treasury records. But as many tribes are frequently in dire need of funds for productive uses, it may be that these funds can be made available to them when appropriations for their benefit cannot be made.

In conclusion it may be said that the result of the establishment of an Indian Claims Commission and its performance of the designated work will be the relief of Congress from the continuous onslaught of bills for jurisdictional acts, the competent advising of Congress on the final disposition of all Indian claims and the quieting of all these claims within a comparatively brief period, and a very decided improvement in the effectiveness of Government work among the Indians.

The CHAIRMAN. Do the members of the committee desire to ask Mr. Poole any questions?

Senator STEIWER. I should like to ask him some questions, Mr. Chairman, if I may.

The CHAIRMAN. Proceed, Senator Steiwer.

Senator STEIWER. I want to call attention first to some language on page 3. It is part of section 2. Starting in line 9, there is a provision that the claims now pending and certain claims not yet filed may be transferred, together with the documents, and so forth. I take it that that language is permissive?

Mr. POOLE. Yes.

Senator STEIWER. It is not intended to require transfer?

Mr. POOLE. That is correct, Senator. I think that is left with the claimant, whether the claim is filed with the Court of Claims.

Senator STEIWER. Yes.

Mr. POOLE. It gives the authority to bring them before this new Commission.

Senator STEIWER. On line 16 there is a phrase, commencing after the word " Commission ", as follows:

And all further proceedings with respect thereto shall be had under the provisions of this act.

That means, I suppose, that in case the claim is transferred—

all further proceedings with respect thereto shall be had under * * * this act.

Mr. POOLE. That is correct. That is, the claimant would not be in a position, if he was dissatisfied with the result of the work of this new Commission, to return to the Court of Claims, from which he had taken his claim.

Sentor STEIWER. Yes. I think probably that meaning is reasonably clear, but I assume there would be no objection to a qualifying word or two. For instance, in line 16, if a semicolon were placed after the word " Commission ", the words " and all " stricken out, and, in lieu of those words, there were included these words " in all cases so transferred ", " further proceedings with respect thereto shall be had under the provisions of this Act ", would not that accomplish your real purpose?

Mr. POOLE. I think perhaps it would if it referred back also to claims previously referred to the Court of Claims by Congress, and not yet filed in such court; but I assume, the way that language is proposed, it would refer to both types of claims.

Senator STEIWER. I suggest that because it occurs to me it might be possible that that last phrase there, commencing " and all further proceedings ", if permitted to stand alone, would carry all claims to the new Commission, even against the objection of claimants in those cases where claims have been filed.

Mr. POOLE. I see. There certainly would be no objection from our standpoint to such an amendment, because it was not meant to mean that.

Senator STEIWER. You made the statement that in 20 cases, as I understood you, the costs were approximately one-half of the amount of the recovery in those cases in which there were successful assertion of a claim.

Mr. POOLE. Yes.

Senator STEIWER. Who pays that cost under the present system?

Mr. DODD. Let me get your statement clear, Senator.

Senator STEIWER. I am referring to the statement Mr. Poole made that in 20 cases, I think he said, the cost of the examination amounted to about one-half of the recovery in those cases, out of the 20 in which success had been attained. Who paid the cost?

Mr. DODD. All of these costs are borne by the Federal Government. That is, where the Accounting Office is called upon to furnish information to the Court of Claims, they are compelled to come to the Congress and get an appropriation and put on additional people to do the work.

Senator STEIWER. Am I right in my understanding that no part of the cost is assessed against the claimant?

Mr. DODD. That is correct; yes.

Mr. POOLE. A case in point is the great *Sioux case* The General Accounting Office were required to put on 80 people, who worked for several years searching records, to determine the amount of that claim.

Senator STEIWER. Under the proposal of the pending bill is it contemplated that there will be any difference in the method of assessing costs?

Mr. POOLE. No.

Senator STEIWER. The costs will be paid by the Government?

Mr. POOLE. That is correct.

Senator STEIWER. And the claimants, the individuals or tribes of Indians who are claimants will pay only such costs as might be incidental to the employment of their ow counsel, and things of that kind?

Mr. POOLE. That is as I understand it.

Senator STEIWER. Those costs are all approved by the Interior Department before they are paid; is that correct?

Mr. DODD. Yes, sir; under the present system they are approved by the Court of Claims.

Senator STEIWER. The attorneys' fees are approved by the Secretary of the Interior, are they not?

Mr. DODD. Most of the jurisdictional bills now authorize the court to fix the fees with the limitation of a certain amount, not to exceed, in most cases, 10 percent.

Senator STEIWER. And there is nothing in this bill that contemplates any change in the system of assessing the cost, either, in such a way as to make it more burdensome to the Indians? That is what I am trying to get at.

Mr. DODD. Absolutely not.

Senator FRAZIER. You stated that the departments were asking for some amendments?

Mr. POOLE. One amendment.

Senator FRAZIER. Where does that come?

Mr. POOLE. In section 2. The different types of claims that may be asserted are enumerated. They are four in number.

Senator STEIWER. Where is the language to which you refer, at the bottom of page 2?

Mr. Poole. It commences on page 2 at line 18 and extends to line 9 on page 3.

We wish to add to that a fifth class. Possibly this fifth class could be included in the broad language of those that are already incorporated in the bill, but we thought, to make it clear—I think it was also suggested by Mr. Grorud—the words " in all claims arising under treaties which have been ratified or executed " be broadened a little by a suggested amendment to read " claims founded upon the Constitution, laws, or treaties of the United States."

Senator Steiwer. In other words, you would broaden the scope some, probably?

Mr. Poole. Yes; we would, because we do not specifically state if the claim was founded on some law of the United States or on a treaty which was ratified.

Senator Steiwer. As so broadened, then, what would be excluded from the scope of this bill; anything?

Mr. Poole. No.

Senator Steiwer. It is your purpose to include every claim?

Mr. Poole. Every conceivable claim.

Senator Steiwer. That might be valid, either in law or in equity?

Mr. Poole. That is right.

Senator Steiwer. And howsoever founded?

Mr. Poole. In addition to that, in order to include claims that would have to rest upon some moral basis, that would have no standing in law or equity.

Senator Steiwer. I note that.

Senator Chavez. Along the lines suggested by the Senator from Oregon, on page 3, line 19, where the bill starts to enumerate the classes of claims that shall not be excluded, coming down to line 23, " on the ground of a prior adjudication with respect thereto in any judicial, administrative, or other proceeding between the same parties ", would not that open the door, if you do not exclude that class of claims, to every claim that has been adjudicated by the Court of Claims?

Mr. Poole. It would, Senator. Now, there is a reason for that.

Senator Chavez. Does the Department of Justice approve of that provision?

Mr. Poole. They made no objection. As I pointed out before, very often these jurisdictional acts were worded in such a fashion that it was impossible for the Court of Claims to give justice to the claimant, requiring him, of necessity, if he were to secure justice, to come back for another jurisdictional act to broaden the base upon which he could assert the claim.

If the Commission is to do a complete job and consider with finality every conceivable claim that a tribe or band could assert, then they should be in a position to take such claims into consideration.

The Chairman. I think oftentimes a hearing before the Court of Claims has developed other claims that have not been known or have not been discovered, even, which makes it necessary to stop the case and go back to Congress for an amendment of the original act or proceed on that claim and complete it and probably go back later on for a new jurisdictional act.

The purpose of this bill, as I understand, is to get these claims into court, get them adjudicated, and get them behind us. On that theory, if something should be developed that was not foreseen in the original jurisdictional act, they could take it up and proceed with it. If some new claim should be found in the prosecution of one claim, the Court of Claims should have jurisdiction over the newly discovered claim; in other words, they should go into the matter fully and make a final adjudication and hope to get the matter adjusted, settled, and out of the way.

Are there any other questions to be asked of Mr. Poole?

Have you someone else to present in behalf of the bill?

Mr. ZIMMERMAN. Mr. Harry Blair, the Assistant Attorney General, is here, and probably wants to speak for the Department of Justice.

The CHAIRMAN. Give your full name to the stenographer, please.

Mr. BLAIR. Harry W. Blair.

The CHAIRMAN. What position do you occupy?

Mr. BLAIR. Assistant Attorney General.

The CHAIRMAN. How long have you held that position?

Mr. BLAIR. Since the 1st of January 1934.

The CHAIRMAN. What work are you assigned to especially?

Mr. BLAIR. Public Lands Division.

The CHAIRMAN. Are you familiar with the bill pending before the committee?

Mr. BLAIR. Yes, sir.

The CHAIRMAN. Proceed to make any statement which you care to, Mr. Blair.

Mr. BLAIR. I just want to say that in the Public Lands Division the cases in the Court of Claims brought by Indian tribes are handled, and therefore we are very familiar with the present status of claims and also with the problems arising when we attempt to expedite the determination of those claims.

We feel that the purpose of this bill is very desirable. We favor the plan. Here is the situation now in the Court of Claims:

There are, as has been stated, 98 cases over there.

The face amount sued for is a little over three and one-quarter million dollars.

The delay in getting action over there is occasioned by the fact that it is necessary, as has been explained, for the General Accounting Office and for the Department of the Interior to make a special investigation of their records, one having to do with financial transactions and the other with general dealings between the Government and the tribe.

I think there is quite a bit of optimism with reference to the question of the time that will be saved on that class of claims. There is only one place to get the testimony and information about a large percentage of these claims, and that is from the Government records. The information and testimony does not exist anywhere else, and it does take several years for the General Accounting Office to go through its records and present a statement of the financial dealings and transactions, running back, frequently, to 1788. That takes years, and it is going to take years with this Commission also.

The advantages of the Commission, as I see it, come from the possibility of the Commission's being able to sift—that is the expression that has been used here—the claims that are worth while from those that are not. Claims generally are divided into three classes or types:

First are the claims that have no basis in fact or in law or in equity or in moral obligation; that is, absolutely worthless claims. There are a great many of those, but many of the tribes feel that they are valid claims. The tribes are entitled to present those claims to somebody that can explain to the tribe, after looking into the matters—it takes usually only a cursory examination—that those claims are worthless, and that there is no chance of ever recovering anything on them. That eliminates a great deal of dead wood in this work, and also gives to the tribes the feeling that they have had their day in court, to an extent, at least.

The second class of claims is those which are wanting in a legal or equitable foundation, but which should appeal to the conscience of the Government, because of some violation by the United States of that rather vague and indefinable rule of good conduct and fair dealing that the Government ought to follow. There are a very large number of those claims which cannot be reached in the Court of Claims or through a jurisdictional act. That is the reason that the Court of Claims apparently comes in for some criticism, which I think is unjust, as to its rulings. It has held, where those matters have arisen, that it has no authority under the several acts, or in any other way, really, to pass upon that type of claim.

The third class of claims, of course, is those which have a basis in law or in equity.

I believe that a commission of the kind contemplated here could sift through these claims and find a great many of them upon which they could make a report direct to the Congress, and the Congress could make an appropriation at once. That would expedite the matter a great deal, and would be a very proper way of reaching the matter.

There is still that class of claims in which there are many questions of law, and in those, of course, the commission could draw and present for the consideration of the Congress a broad, comprehensive, fair jurisdictional act that would give the Court of Claims an opportunity to go into the merits of the several claims involved.

There is the objection that has been spoken of as made by the Department to one provision of the bill: The bill provides that the finding of the Commission shall be taken as prima facie evidence where it makes a finding of fact when the case reaches the Court of Claims. We think it is manifestly unfair to a court to ask it to pass upon a state of facts where it has before it the evidence on which that finding of fact is made, and the court deems that on that very same testimony there should be a different finding of fact. There is no provision in the bill and there is no way of knowing whether the taking of the testimony presented to this Commission will be governed by rules of evidence or how the evidence will be presented.

As a simple illustration, suppose that oral testimony should be received by the Commission involving some treaty along in the fifties or sixties. It necessarily would be of someone who was very young at the time and could not have any knowledge that would be accepted by a court. The possibility might be that it would be, but it is seemingly a remote possibility. If the Commission should base its finding of fact upon testimony of that kind, opinion and tribal tradition, that a court would not think sufficiently good, then the Court of Claims' hands would be tied in passing upon that finding of fact.

That is the basis of the objection that has been made to that one phrase.

Senator STEIWER. Do you suggest modification, Mr. Blair, or elimination of it?

Mr. BLAIR. I suggest the elimination of that word, merely the elimination of the statement at the bottom of page 4, the last sentence, lines 23, 24, and 25.

Senator STEIWER. You would delete that whole sentence?

Mr. BLAIR. As I say, the Department of Justice feels that the bill is one which, either in its present form or with whatever modifications the committee thinks proper, is a desirable bill. The establishment of such a commission is a desirable thing, in our judgment.

The CHAIRMAN. The committee will now stand adjourned, subject to the call of the chair, for further hearings on this bill.

(Whereupon, at 12:03 p. m., the committee adjourned, subject to the call of the chair.)

INDIAN CLAIMS COMMISSION ACT

MONDAY, JUNE 10, 1935

UNITED STATES SENATE,
COMMITTEE ON INDIAN AFFAIRS,
Washington, D. C.

The committee met, pursuant to call, at 10:30 a. m., in room 424, Senate Office Building, Hon. Elmer Thomas (chairman) presiding.

The CHAIRMAN. At the last meeting some testimony was given in behalf of S. 2731. At this time I will ask Mr. Collier, the Commissioner of Indian Affairs, if he has any further suggestions to make on behalf of the bill.

STATEMENT OF HON. JOHN COLLIER, COMMISSIONER OF INDIAN AFFAIRS

Mr. COLLIER. I do not think so, Mr. Chairman. There have been hearings in the House which did not develop any opposition. There remains only one point of controversy, I believe, which is the paragraph at the bottom of page 4, reading:

In all proceedings brought pursuant hereto in the Court of Claims all determinations of facts by the Commission shall be accorded prima facie weight.

The Department of Justice has suggested that instead the findings be merely admitted as evidence, without being accorded prima facie weight. On that we find ourselves not in agreement with the Department. They may be right, but we think that prima facie weight should be given to the findings.

Mr. Blair is here to explain the Department of Justice view, as is Mr. Stormont.

STATEMENT OF HON. HARRY W. BLAIR, ASSISTANT ATTORNEY GENERAL

The CHAIRMAN. Does the Department of Justice care to make any further statement in regard to this provision on page 4?

Mr. BLAIR. I think not, Mr. Chairman, with regard to that particular provision. At the hearing the other day I gave the reason that was given by the Department in a letter to the Budget Bureau; that is to say, that when a finding of facts is made by the commission and it goes to the Court of Claims under an act which provides that it shall be prima facie evidence of the state of facts set forth, then the Court of Claims would be prohibited from looking at the evidence and saying that the facts stated were not borne out by the evidence heard by the Commission. As I said, there is nothing in the bill that fixes any rules of evidence to be followed by the Commission, and, therefore, the Commission could make a finding of facts based upon incompetent and immaterial evidence, and the court would be bound by that finding of facts. That is the point raised by the Department.

Mr. COLLIER. Might I ask Mr. Blair to elucidate to my lay and unlegal mind this: The effect of the word "prima facie" is not to exclude the introduction of contrary testimony, is it?

Mr. BLAIR. Oh, no, no.

Mr. COLLIER. It may be impeached?

Mr. BLAIR. It would necessitate the introduction of additional testimony in order that the court might change the finding of facts. If no additional testimony were introduced, the court would be bound by the finding of the Commission.

Mr. COLLIER. But if the Government, for example, were in dissent, the Government could introduce the original evidence, or if the Indian tribe were in dissent, it could introduce the additional evidence, could it not?

Mr. BLAIR. If there were additional evidence?

Mr. COLLIER. If there be no additional evidence, is it not a case of "that is that"?

Mr. BLAIR. If there is no additional evidence, the court is bound by the findings of the Commission as to the facts. That is the point. That finding of facts might be made upon the basis of testimony which a court would not accept as competent, relevant, and material evidence. That is the only point.

Mr. COLLIER. Would the effect of altering the language to read as the Department of Justice proposes be, as a practical matter, to practically insure that every case would be retried in its details by the court?

Mr. BLAIR. I think so.

Mr. COLLIER. It would do that?

Mr. BLAIR. If the finding of facts by the Commission was such a finding and based upon such testimony that the court deemed the finding of facts could not stand, it seems to us that a court ought not to have its hands tied, as it were, in reaching a conclusion and a judgment in the case.

Mr. COLLIER. Another possible procedure, Mr. Blair, is this, that the whole of those three lines be stricken from the bill. Suppose they were not in there at all: In what condition would that leave things?

Mr. BLAIR. Then the court could give such weight to the report as it deemed proper in the hearing of the case, just as any other evidence. I would not favor particularly striking out those three lines, but merely changing the last line, 25, so that it would read:

shall be accorded such weight as the court may deem proper;

leave it up to the court.

Mr. COLLIER. Is not that practically the same thing as striking them out? If you struck them out entirely it would be the same as if you amended it this way, would it not?

Mr. BLAIR. Not exactly.

Mr. COLLIER. But still there is a certain value in keeping it.

Mr. BLAIR. I think there is value in keeping it in there. As a practical matter, of course, the findings of fact made by the Commission, we must presume, will be based upon competent and proper testimony; but the chance that they might not be is all that I am bringing to the attention of the committee.

Mr. COLLIER. Is not this also the case, Mr. Blair, that a given case would go into the Court of Claims under a special jurisdictional act—will it not?

Mr. BLAIR. Prepared by the Commission.

Mr. COLLIER. Yes. In any given instance, if Congress wanted to give prima facie weight——

Mr. BLAIR. Oh, it could say so.

Mr. COLLIER (continuing). It could say so; and that would override this.

Mr. BLAIR. Exactly.

Mr. COLLIER. So that if the Department of Justice carries its point, it does not foreclose the introduction of the prima facie weight in given cases hereafter?

Mr. BLAIR. Oh, no; no.

Mr. COLLIER. I do not think that the issue is one over which we ought to lock horns at all, Mr. Chairman.

Mr. BLAIR. An instance of that situation might be, Mr. Chairman, that in a hearing before the Commission affidavits might be presented and accepted by the Commission. If a report and finding of fact were based upon affidavits, the court might or might not be willing to accept the conclusion of facts based upon affidavits. However, the Congress, in the jurisdictional act sending it to the Court of Claims, could provide that the report should be accepted as prima facie evidence, which would exclude that question there.

Mr. COLLIER. I believe, Mr. Chairman, that there is no other material point on which argument has arisen except this one point. I certainly would not be inclined to stand out for the contention of the Department, although I believe Mr. Poole, who is not here because he is meeting with the House committee on the same subject now, feels more strongly about it than I do. But certainly I do not see that it has supreme importance.

The CHAIRMAN. It is your opinion that lines 23, 24, and 25, on page 4, could be removed from the bill without injury to the measure?

Mr. COLLIER. Instead of that the language proposed by the Department of Justice might be more advisable, wherein prima facie weight is taken away, but it shall be accepted as evidence.

The CHAIRMAN. If you take out the words " prima facie ", then the three lines are meaningless, as I see it.

Mr. COLLIER. That is what I think. Is that correct, Mr. Blair, in your judgment?

Mr. BLAIR. Perhaps so. My thought was that if the bill itself provided that the finding of fact should go to the court and should be considered by the court it would be helpful; and, therefore, that if the bill provided that the findings of facts should go to the court and should be given such weight as the court might deem proper it would be all right, because otherwise the Court of Claims might hold that it had no authority at all to give any credence or any weight to this finding of fact. It might be able, if that provision were in there, to form its judgment based on that finding of fact without doing anything further. So, admitting that finding of facts was correct or proper, under the authority of that clause it could base its judgment right on that finding of facts and conclude the matter at once, otherwise it might have to go and take a lot of testimony.

Senator FRAZIER. If there were no new testimony to be offered, why should not they base their findings on that?

Mr. BLAIR. They should base it on that, but without a provision in the bill that it could do so the court might conclude that it did not have that authority.

Mr. COLLIER. That is what I am unable to make out—that if there be new facts they can be presented; but in the absence of new facts, then and then only would the findings of the Commission be conclusive, as I see it. In the absence of new facts, why should they not be conclusive?

Mr. BLAIR. Because the findings of facts might be based upon testimony that the court would deem not proper, legitimate, relevant, and competent testimony.

The CHAIRMAN. Prima facie means that the allegations are to be taken as admitted unless objected to and counter testimony submitted sufficient to outweigh the facts alleged to be prima facie. I see no difference between your position and that of Mr. Collier. I would like for you gentlemen to get together and submit the language that you want in this bill, because this is a bill to be operated by the two departments.

Mr. COLLIER. I would much rather let the committee decide and myself not be too insistent, because, after all, this is a minor point.

MEMORANDUM SUBMITTED BY RUFUS G. POOLE, ASSISTANT SOLICITOR OF THE DEPARTMENT OF THE INTERIOR, WITH REFERENCE TO THE AMENDMENT PROPOSED BY THE ATTORNEY GENERAL TO THE INDIAN CLAIMS COMMISSION BILL

The amendment to section 3, paragraph 2, of the Indian Claims Commission bill, proposed by the Attorney General of the United States in a letter to the Director General of the Budget, and set forth as recommended by the Director General in the report on the bill by the Interior Department, would change that section to read as follows:

In all proceedings brough pursuant hereto in the Court of Claims all determination of fact by the Commission shall be admissible in evidence, but may be reviewed by the court either on the basis of evidence taken before the Commission, or on additional evidence, or both.

The present section is of different tenor:

In all proceedings brought pursuant hereto in the Court of Claims, all determination of fact by the Commission shall be accorded prima facie weight.

The change proposed is vital since, by removing the weight to be accorded the Commission's determination of facts when a claim acted upon by the Commission is presented to the Court of Claims, it undermines the importance and prestige of the Commission and lessens its effectiveness and potential economy. The Solicitor's office regards such an amendment as undesirable and bases its objections on the following considerations:

(1) The proposed amendment is based upon the apprehension that the provision according prima facie weight to the determinations of fact by the Commission will prevent the Court of Claims from reviewing or overriding the Commission's findings. This apprehension is not justified in view of the plain meaning of the phrase and the repeated explanation and interpretation by the courts of similar uses of the phrase.

(2) Moreover, while the legal effect of the proposed amendment is not entirely clear, it will apparently allow in the Court of Claims a trial de novo of the facts, thus setting no value whatsoever on the determinations arrived at by the special fact-finding commission, and in effect reducing the Commission from a fact-finding to a purely investigatory agency whose findings are merely evidence of the facts and no more.

(3) Even if the words of the proposed amendment would not of themselves compel such slight value to be placed upon the Commission's work, the fact that the provision for prima-facie weight originally proposed to Congress had been removed by the congressional committees would argue conclusively an intent by Congress to deny any weight to the findings of the Commission. Because of the damage to the Commission possible from such legislative history, the Solicitor's office would disfavor the weakening of the prima facie provision in any way, or its elimination by the committees of Congress.

(4) The ultimate result of such an amendment would be to weaken the Commission in the eyes of Congress, of the Court of Claims, of the litigants, and of the Commission itself, thus making unlikely any final disposition of Indian claims by that agency.

A further discussion of each of these objections to the amendment follows, particularly with a view to making clear the legal meaning and implications of the prima facie provision and the proposed amendment.

(1) Normally, when a statute creates a Commission to determine facts, it is contemplated that its findings of fact within its province will be conclusive when supported by evidence, and the courts accord such finality to its findings even when this was not specifically required by the statute (*Dahlstrom Metallic Door Co.* v. *Industrial Board,* 284 U. S. 594). (See *Crowell* v. *Benson,* 285 U. S. 22, 46–50; *II Wigmore, Evidence,* 2d Ed. 1933, secs. 1347, 1355.) The respect accorded the determinations of the great number of administrative commissions set up in recent years amply testifies to this fact. It is only when the legislature desires to be unusually cautious that it provides that the findings of the Commission shall be prima-facie evidence of the facts when the case comes into court, rather than final determinations. This provision was included in this bill in order to allow the Court of Claims to hear additional evidence and to review the findings of the Commission where good cause was shown, as desired by the Department of Justice. This provision is also found in section 16(2) of the Transportation Act of 1920, which provides that on the trial of a suit to enforce a reparation order of the Interstate Commerce Commission, "the findings and order of the Commission shall be prima-facie evidence of the facts therein stated." It is by referring to the leading cases interpreting this provision that the meaning of the prima-facie provision becomes most clear.

In the first place, this provision means that in the absence of evidence introduced by the defendant to attack the validity of the findings, the findings of the Commission must be presumed to have been justified by the evidence before the Commission, and to state the true facts which the court can accept as a basis for its decision (*Meeker* v. *Lehigh Valley R. Co.,* 236 U. S. 412). This is the first point at which the present section is superior to that proposed by the Department of Justice. Under the present section, unless the parties themselves introduce substantial evidence to attack the findings, the findings have sufficient weight to be considered by the court as correct and final determinations of fact and no further investigation is necessary. However, if such findings are made merely evidence of the facts, the court must make an independent investigation into the evidence and record before the Commission to determine what reliability and credibility can be attached to it, no matter how excellent the work of the Commission may have been.

The words suggested in the proposed amendment, " admissible in evidence " can mean only " shall be evidence of the facts " and nothing more. There is no doubt that under the present section the findings of the Commission would be admissible. *Cf. Meeker & Co.* v. *Lehigh Valley R. Co.* (the second *Meeker case*), (236 U. S. 434). Nor is there any doubt that under the prima-facie provision additional evidence not before the Commission would be admissible to attack the correctness of the determination. The defendant is always free to introduce additional evidence; his only problem is to produce evidence sufficiently compelling to overthrow the presumption in favor of the determination. For these reasons the prima-facie provision has been called chiefly a change in the burden of proof upon the parties (the *Meeker case, supra; Pennsylvania R. R. Co.* v. *Weber*, 257 U. S. 85; *II Wigmore, evidence, supra*, sec. 1356).

But the problem apparently uppermost in the Attorney General's considerations is the extent to which the Court of Claims can review the findings of the Commission in the light of the evidence before it. His expressed desire is to allow the Court of Claims to determine the "weight of the evidence before the Commission" (letter of the Attorney General to the Director General of the Budget, May 24, 1935, forwarded on May 31, 1935, by the Assistant Director to the Secretary of the Interior). This is the second point at which the present section differs from the proposed amendment.

Under the prima-facie provision a court is free to review the evidence before the Commission to discover whether the finding is based upon any inaccuracies, or, more broadly, whether the finding is based upon substantial evidence", whenever the testimony and record before the Commission is placed on evidence by the opponent of the finding. In *Pennsylvania R. R. Co.* v. *Weber* (257 U. S. 85), the defendant put in evidence at the trial the evidence which had been before the Interstate Commerce Commission and additional evidence to assist in combatting the Commission's determination of damages. The trial court found the Commission had used an erroneous method of computation and itself found the amount of damages, and was sustained by the Supreme Court. There are numerous other cases where the defendant freely put in both types of evidence to challenge the Commission's findings. See, e. g., *Southern Ry. Co.* v. *St. Louis Hay Co.* (214 U. S. 297) ; *Krauss Bros. Lumber Co.* v. *Mellon* (18 Fed. (2d) 369; C. C. A. 5th, 1927) ; *Clark Bros. Coal Mining Co.* v. *Pennsylvania R. R. Co.* (238 Fed. 642; D. C. Pa. 1916). In several cases the defendant relied solely upon the evidence before the Commission to prove the lack of basis for the Commission's findings, introducing no additional evidence, and such reliance was upheld by the courts who examined that evidence independently. *Speller* v. *Atcheson, T. & S. F. Ry. Co.* (253 U. S. 117, 1920) ; *Pennsylvania R. R. Co.* v. *W. F. Jacoby* (242 U. S. 89, 1916). The usual procedure is for the plaintiff to introduce the formal findings and order of the Interstate Commerce Commission awarding him damages and for the defendant thereupon to introduce the record of the testimony before the Commission and any relevant exhibits, asserting the insufficiency of the evidence. When the defendant thus presents the record before the Commission, it is not only the privilege but the duty of the trial court to investigate the record and determine whether the finding was sufficiently supported by the evidence (*Michigan Central Railroad Co.* v. *Elliott*, 256 Fed. 18; C. C. A. 2d, 1919).

However, the question litigated in these cases is whether there was sufficient or "substantial" evidence before the Commission to support the findings, not whether the finds were supported by the "weight of the evidence." The courts repeatedly assert that they are not concerned with the question whether the evidence before the Interstate Commerce Commission would be satisfactory to all reasonable minds, or with the strength of its probative force or with the possibility that on the same evidence they would have come to a different conclusion. *Speller* v. *Atchison, T. & S. F. Ry Co., supra; Montrose Oil Refining Co.* v. *St. Louis, S. F. Ry. Co.* (25 Fed. (2d) 750; N. D. Tex., 1927) ; aff'd 25 Fed. (2d) 755, C. C. A. 5th, 1928. This attitude is universally taken by courts when the case before them rests upon the findings of a commission empowered to determine facts in given circumstances. Except in the case of jurisdictional facts a person has no right to have facts determined by a commission, or even by a master in chancery or advisory commissioners, redetermined by a court on the same evidence where that evidence supports the finding made simply because a different conclusion is possible or even more apparent. See *Crowel* v. *Benson* (285 U. S. 22, 46–50).

(2) Therefore, when the Attorney General suggests that the determination by the Court of Claims of the weight of the evidence before the Claims Commission should be allowed, he is reducing the Claims Commission to a low level

of authority not shared even by pure advisers to the courts. The proposed amendment would accomplish that result, since no weight is attached to the Commission's determinations. The Commission, through its findings, would come before the court like any ordinary witness with its evidentiary weight and credibility to be determined as the court pleases. Since the proposed amendment can mean only that the Court of Claims can decide for itself what weight to give the evidence before the Commission, this is, in fact, a trial de novo, since old and new evidence are admitted and no limitation is placed upon the court as a result of the Commission's exercise of discretion. While this is, in all probability, the effect of the language proposed, the language is peculiarly unfortunate, since to "review" findings on the basis of additional evidence is an unnatural procedure and raises many technical legal questions.

In summary of points 1 and 2 it may be said that under the present section much of the ability to attack the Claims Commission findings desired by the Attorney General will be permitted. In fact, following the words of the proposed amendment, the findings of the Commission will be admissible in evidence, and will be able to be reviewed by the court upon the evidence before the Commission, and may be attacked by additional evidence without any change in the present language. But the proposed change of language will work an injurious change of substance, since, by providing no weight to be accorded the findings, it requires the court to determine the weight of the findings in all cases by weighing the evidence before the Commission and by reexamining all the evidence in the case.

(3) Since the language of the proposed amendment is ambiguous, it becomes highly probable that the Court of Claims, and, in fact, all persons interested, will refer to the legislative history of the act to determine the significance of the language. When it is perceived that this provision originally placed prima facie weight upon the findings and that this provision was withdrawn, the natural conclusion will be that outlined above, that the Court of Claims may disregard the Commission's findings. It is obvious that any other weakening or elimination of the provision would invite the same conclusion.

(4) A commission which merely collects evidence is entirely inadequate to solve the difficulties in the settling of Indian claims. Lawyers and Government bureaus now fulfill that function. What is needed is the final determination of those claims which because of their political nature cannot be decided in the Court of Claims and the determination of the facts in all cases in such a way so that Congress and the Court of Claims may rely upon them in making settlements and decisions. Unless a specific provision is included giving weight to the determinations of the Commission, litigants will slight its work and Congress and the court will not feel justified in leaning upon its findings. New facts and considerations will be pressed upon the congressional committees, and the court and Indian claims will remain, as now, troublesome and endlessly agitated controversies.

Memorandum for Mr. Grorud relative to Indian Claims Commission bill.

In response to your telephone message beg to suggest:

The bill on page 4, lines 23 to 25, inclusive, provides that " In all proceedings brought pursuant hereto in the Court of Claims, all determinations of fact by the Commission shall be accorded prima facie weight."

We feel that this sentence should be amended to read:

" In all proceedings brought pursuant hereto in the Court of Claims, all determinations of fact by the Commission may be considered and reviewed by the Court of Claims and given such weight as the court shall deem proper."

The bill directs the Commission to ascertain and determine all facts and make report thereon to the Congress. In the performance of this duty the Commission is authorized to make thorough search for all evidence affecting the claims presented and to take oral testimony. The bill does not provide or require that the examination of witnesses or evidence received shall be in accordance with the rules of law. That there be no requirements in this regard is no doubt advisable in the case of a mere investigating commission, the duty of which it is to inquire into not only legal or equitable claims but claims which appeal to the conscience of the sovereign.

With respect to the latter class, which are entirely outside the field of law, it is probably wise not to impose upon the Commission the rules of evidence which obtain in a court. But where the claim under investigation has as its basis the alleged violation of some legal or equitable right and as a result of the Commission's investigation, the claim finds its way into the Court of Claims, the situation is very different. Such a claim, and the evidence supporting it, should in all respects conform with the rules of law or equity. The investigating commission, unhampered by the rules of evidence, might very conceivably reach a conclusion of fact upon a record composed of incompetent, irrelevant, and immaterial evidence. Such a conclusion of fact could not be sustained in a court of law. It is for this reason that we believe that the bill should not provide that the conclusions of fact shall be given prima facie weight, i. e., weight which it takes evidence to alter. There might not be any other evidence. Under our proposed amendment the Court of Claims can consider the conclusion of fact together with the record upon which it is based. If the record consists of competent and relevant evidence, the conclusion would no doubt be adopted by the court, and additional evidence would be required to overturn it. If the record, on the contrary, consisted of incompetent and immaterial evidence, the Court of Claims could refuse to follow the conclusion and it would then be incumbent upon the party interested to establish his case by competent evidence adduced before the court. This proposed amendment simply permits either party, the United States or the Indian tribe, to contest in the Court of Claims determinations of fact which are believed not to be sustained by the record made before the Commission.

HARRY W. BLAIR,
Assistant Attorney General.

The CHAIRMAN. Mr. Arnold has submitted an amendment. On page 2, line 12, after the word " band " insert the following language: "or class having a common right or claim ".

The purpose evidently is to extend the opportunity for filing claims to a smaller number of Indians than a tribe or a band, by providing that a few Indians having a common right or claim might submit such claim.

Has the Department any suggestion to make as to the advisability of having that amendment?

Mr. COLLIER. The only reason that occurs to me why it might be inadvisable would be that it would permit a small group of Indians with individual claims to form themselves into such a class, which would force the adjudication of these innumerable individual claims into the Commission. The Commission has a big job, anyhow.

Senator FRAZIER. Unless something of that kind is included, how are these little bands that are away from the tribe to be taken care of?

Mr. COLLIER. The bands are covered in " tribe, band, or other communal group." However, say there are three or four allottees who have a grievance and who have received patents in fee. They could not just band together into a group of litigants and come together before the Commission. There is no objection to their coming except that it would enormously increase the labors of the Commission.

The CHAIRMAN. As I understand the theory of this bill, it is not intended to give individual Indians a right to come into court; is that correct?

Mr. COLLIER. Not as drawn. If that were done, certainly the court would have to be indefinitely enlarged, so that they could handle all that business.

The CHAIRMAN. If this bill should become a law as now drawn, it would force upon the Commission a responsibility in the earlier stages of its existence to define " tribe " and define " band ", so it will be up to the Commission itself to say just how many Indians and what kind of Indians would be necessary to form a tribe, and the same thing as regarding forming a band.

Mr. COLLIER. I do not know why these Choctaws would not come right under the Commission. They are a segregated group. If they are now by themselves, the fact they were once parties to a treaty in common with the Oklahoma Choctaws would not be relevant. They certainly are a communal group, and they would come right under this bill.

STATEMENT OF J. E. ARNOLD

Mr. ARNOLD. Are the Mississippi Choctaws considered a group or a band?

Mr. COLLIER. They are that, quite definitely so.

Mr. ARNOLD. Has that been determined? It is an undetermined question.

Mr. COLLIER. It is a question that this Commission would resolve, and it would resolve, it seems to me, in the affirmative; certainly it would. They have definitely a collective interest. They all suffered together, did they not?

Mr. ARNOLD. I hardly agree with you, but that interest has not been determined. The object of that amendment is to bring them before this Cimmission.

Mr. COLLIER. I think they are before the Commission. The trouble with that amendment is that that brings not only them before the Commission but any number of other individual claimants of all sorts and kinds.

Mr. ARNOLD. We might find a difference of opinion when the Commission is created.

Mr. COLLIER. If you want to get them in, put in a specific reference to the Choctaws, but do not adopt omnibus language that will bring in all the individual cases before the Commission.

Mr. ARNOLD. What about the smaller groups of Indians in Polk County, Tex.? There are two or three groups down there.

Mr. COLLIER. They certainly are a group. Look at California. There we have a case where all the Indians are involved in one litigation, but that does not mean that any one of the scores of particular tribes or bands in California may not have claims over and above what they are litigating now. It would certainly come before this Commission. It certainly does not mean, for example, that only the Sioux Tribe as a whole could appear before the Commission. Any settlement of the Sioux Tribe could appear before the Commission, because it is a communal group. I am certain, in the case of the Mississippi Choctaws, they would be defined as a communal group.

Mr. ARNOLD. The object of this amendment was to broaden the litigation so that there would not be any hair splitting.

Mr. COLLIER. There would not be any hair splitting, but I do not know why you should broaden it by any definition that would allow any two Indians with individual claims just to get together, and then they can force the Commission to dispose of all these hundreds of thousands of matters of individual Indian business, unless the **committee wants to do** that. If you are going to do that, you have to create more machinery; if it is to become an agency for settling individual claims as well as these group claims, then it has to be enormously increased in personnel.

Mr. ARNOLD. There is a group of those Choctaws in Louisiana.

The CHAIRMAN. It is obvious that the word "band" is intended to mean a fewer number of Indians than a tribe.

Mr. ARNOLD. Yes.

The CHAIRMAN. A band of Indians really might be a group of Indians belonging to different tribes, if they happened to live in the same section of the country—Siouxs, Choctaws, Chickasaws, Creeks, and whatnot. They might not belong to any one particular tribe, any more than one or two of them, but banded together they would constitute a band of Indians. So it occurs to me that until we have a definition of the word "band" it will not be necessary to try to define a smaller group, because a band of Indians could be a very small number.

Mr. ARNOLD. Pardon me. I believe the Court of Claims has defined that word "band" somewhere.

The CHAIRMAN. Under the terms of this bill it would be up to the court immediately to define "band" if the request were raised. Until the courts have determined or defined the term, it might be advisable to let this stand, because it might be determined in such a way as to satisfy all the Indians who were to come in.

Mr. COLLIER. Certainly the Seminoles of Florida, who were once part of the Seminoles of Oklahoma, are now a band, at least, and a communal group. They would come in here in a hurry with their own claims, that have been accumulating long since they were split off from the Oklahoma Indians.

Senator FRAZIER. There are several bands in Florida.

The CHAIRMAN. At least three different groups.

Mr. COLLIER. And they might have separate claims.

Senator FRAZIER. Under your definition of this, each one of those bands would be eligible to come in under this bill?

Mr. COLLIER. Oh, yes; I think surely they would.

The CHAIRMAN. I think the language of the amendment is intended only to define the term "band." I believe that the word "band" is broad enough to cover the language of the amendment. It occurs to me that when the court has a chance to pass upon it and a chance to define it, then, if this definition is not satisfactory, sometime in the future we can take up an amendment to define the term "band" in such a way as to satisfy those who might be out of court, if advisable.

Mr. ARNOLD. All right, Senator. The only object of that amendment was that we would not have any quibbling or hairsplitting in coming before the Commission.

The CHAIRMAN. It would be a matter of proof, anyway, either under the wording of the amendment or under the word "band." I believe you would have a better chance under the word "band." For the present, it occurs to me this is broad enough, until we find it is not.

Mr. BLAIR. May I ask a question, please, Mr. Chairman? The term "band" has been defined at one time by the Court of Claims, indicating a group of Indians belonging to a particular tribe, smaller than the tribe, but which has been recognized by the Government, as a band or as a particular group, as a part of a tribe. This bill refers to " or other communal group." The question I wanted to ask is: Does that mean a communal group composed of all of one tribe, or a communal group composed of various tribes, so located geographically as to form a group?

Mr. COLLIER. Yes. It was intended to go even beyond the definition of " band ", but your question is a little broad, because it means the Government or any branch has negotiated with that group. That alone would bring the Mississippi Choctaws into it. There may be other cases of groups of Indians who have a common grievance, who have suffered a common loss of land through laches or error of the Government. It is intended that they, if only a local village, shall be able to come in.

Mr. BLAIR. Regardless of that tribal relation?

Mr. COLLIER. Yes. The communal group is intended to go very much further than the definition of " band." I am confident it will bring all these legitimate cases in.

The CHAIRMAN. Let me give two illustrations that will serve to make clear the point that you raise. In my section of Oklahoma we have three different groups of Indians that have the same legal rights, the Kiowas, Comanches, and Apaches. The three tribes are joined together in a certain area, and they all stand on an equality before the law. Their lands were disposed of at one time, and they were joined together, and they participated together in the returns from the sale of their lands. From the date that they were so joined to the present their rights are common.

Now, we might have a few Apaches, a few Comanches, and a few Kiowas form a band. Their rights would all be the same, but it would be a smaller number than either tribe.

Then take in northern Oklahoma we have the Wichitas, the Caddos, and various bands, about 13 different tribes, remnants of different tribes, associated there on an equality before the law. A few of those Indians of each tribe might get together. Their rights would be in common, but they might not be satisfied with what was given to the larger group, and they would want to prosecute a claim for the benefit of the smaller group. That is what I had in mind by stating that a number of Indians of different tribes might get together. I doubt if you could take a Choctaw and a Seminole and a Creek, all having a different status before the law, and put them into a group and give them the right to go into the Court of Claims. I cannot conceive of any case they might have. But where fewer Indians than a tribe, or a group of tribes, have a common status before the law, I do think they ought to have the right to come in and assert the claim. Through that they might open up a case and bring in a larger number. That might be possible.

Senator STEIWER. Can the chairman advise the committee whether it was the purpose of the author of the bill to exclude consideration of claims of individual Indians?

The CHAIRMAN. We just mentioned that before you came in, Senator Steiwer. Mr. Collier stated that if that were done, it would necessitate a very substantial increase in the personnel of the court and the business of the court.

Senator STEIWER. That is, if individual claims were not permitted within the jurisdiction of the Commission?

The CHAIRMAN. Yes; and the bill was not drawn to authorize the court to entertain individual claims, the smallest number being a band.

Senator STEIWER. I think that point would be well taken, that it would impose a very great burden upon the Commission if it were charged with the responsibility of examining individual claims.

While I have interrupted, may I ask what is the significance of the word " communal " in line 12?

Mr. COLLIER. It simply means a community. It is an attempt to go beyond the limitations of the meaning of " band ", which has been imposed by this single definition, and to take a simple group of Indians who have a common interest, who have suffered a common injury, but who may not heretofore have been recognized by any branch of the Government.

There is a big group of Indians, the Croatans, as they are called, down in North Carolina. It is not certain that they could qualify as a band, because never heretofore has the Government recognized them in any way; yet there are thousands of them. They are a communal group.

Senator STEIWER. Do you feel if you used the word " group " without any qualifying word you would take in more territory than you would want to take in?

Mr. COLLIER. You might, because that might throw you over to the people who have made themselves into a group, a lot of individual claimants who had formed themselves into a group merely in order to get into this court.

Senator STEIWER. Yes; a small, miscellaneous group.

Mr. COLLIER. Yes; because I doubt if there is a case anywhere where an Indian has a claim that he cannot find another Indian that has that kind of a claim. It would be merely the lumping of that kind of claims. We do not want these innumerable, heterogeneous Indian claims put on the doorstep of the court if we can help it. Some qualifying word—maybe " communal " is not the right word— which indicates a historic identity, or an identity of habitat, makes the thing a communal group, a group with historic identity, and not just a detached group of people who got together and made out they were a group so as to get into this court.

Senator STEIWER. The essential thing is that they have a common claim, is it not?

Mr. COLLIER. Yes; a common claim of a group character.

The CHAIRMAN. Does anyone have any further suggestions to make for the record relative to the merits or demerits of the bill pending before the committee?

Senator DONAHEY. I would like to suggest, if I may, that by section 3 the Commission is given certain duties to perform, certain reports to make. Why would it not be good to attach to that section 3 that they shall keep a record, and all claims accepted or rejected or acts of the Commission shall be by a yea-and-nay vote. That way we can find out who is who on these commissions and what they are voting for. In some of our hearings it was developed that a commission of five members was not required to keep a journal. When we were making an examination at the hearing of some of the rights, it was found there was no record of how the commission had voted. Had we had a journal, and had the acts been by yea and nay, we would have known what the acts were from the record. Such a provision would not do the claimants any harm.

Senator FRAZIER. I think that is a good suggestion.

Mr. COLLIER. I think that is a good suggestion, too.

Senator FRAZIER. Mr. Ralph Case, an attorney here in the city who has handled a number of Indian claims, and who has some claims pending in the Court of Claims at the present time, was here last Monday, and was to come today, but I do not see him. He suggested a couple of amendments, on page 3.

On page 3, line 14, after the word " complainant ", insert " in cases not yet filed in said court ", which just clarifies the language.

Then, in line 19, after the words " Court of Claims ", put in a colon and insert:

Provided, That in cases now pending in the Court of Claims, the transfer thereof to the Commission shall be made upon motion of the attorney of record in each case, with the approval of the Secretary of the Interior.

That is where a case is now pending and a great deal of work has been done on it, it would be up to the attorney of record, with the approval of the Secretary of the Interior, to say how it should be handled.

Mr. COLLIER. A case already in the Court of Claims?

Senator FRAZIER. Yes; and which has been there probably for several years, and a great deal of work done on it.

The CHAIRMAN. Does the amendment state whether or not the motion is to be made by the attorney for the claimant or the attorney for the Government?

Senator FRAZIER. Here is the proviso the way he has it:

Provided, That in cases now pending in the Court of Claims the transfer thereof to the Commission shall be made upon motion of the attorney of record in each case with the approval of the Secretary of the Interior.

Mr. COLLIER. Suppose the Government wanted to try it out?

Mr. BLAIR. The attorney of record for the claimant?

Senator FRAZIER. Yes.

Mr. COLLIER. Might not the Government desire to transfer it also?

Mr. BLAIR. I do not see that we would. I think the clause is desirable, because it would be unfair to the attorneys for these tribes who have gotten the case into the Court of Claims almost ready for decision to have it ruthlessly taken out of that court and given to the Commission, which would delay it 2 or 3 years more.

Senator FRAZIER. That was Mr. Case's argument.

Mr. BLAIR. Yes; that is correct.

Senator FRAZIER. That there are some of the cases now practically ready for decision.

The CHAIRMAN. It occurs to me that this should be clarified as to making it specific. If it is intended to permit either side to transfer the case or to move for transfer, the amendment should so state. If it is intended to be limited only to attorneys for the claimant, it should so state.

Senator FRAZIER. I think that is what he meant.

Mr. COLLIER. Mr. Blair seems to think that that is satisfactory to the Government, and, that point of view being adopted, then this additional language would be competent.

STATEMENT OF FRANK J. BOUDINOT, ATTORNEY

Mr. BOUDINOT. On that same amendment I have prepared and would like to have made part of the record at this same place and the same point a suggested amendment. The amendment I have prepared and would like to submit reads as follows. After those words insert the following:

Provided, That any and all claims on which petitions heretofore have been filed in the Court of Claims may be transferred to the Commission on motion of the attorney of record for the Indian claimants with the approval of the Secretary of the Interior; and in any and all such claims so transferred the attorney or attorneys heretofore and now representing the claimant Indians in the Court of Claims shall continue as attorney or attorneys for the said Indians in all further proceedings before the Commission, the committees of Congress, and before any court, officer, or authority having at any time any duty or power in the premises, with the same powers, authority, responsibilities, and duties they now have, so far as applicable, until final determination and settlement of all claims so transferred.

The CHAIRMAN. Your amendment would open the question to many complications. That would mean that on claims which have been pending for years, where various attorneys have had contracts from time to time and have done some work, those attorneys would be automatically recognized by the Commission as attorneys of record, and their authority would be continued to prosecute the case, whether or not they were working harmoniously or otherwise.

Mr. COLLIER. I think that is a modification of existing law. Under the present law and theory of the law the court is supposed to insist upon prosecution and celerity of action at any time. The question may be raised as to the fitness of an attorney. Moreover, the Indians may raise it. That imports, it seems to me, something entirely foreign to the question.

Senator STEIWER. The objection I see to it is that it imposes a statutory definition and creates a statutory right in the attorneys that might not be consistent with justice to all concerned. I am in favor of some such amendment as was suggested here by Senator Frazier that is not too inelastic, and would permit the Secretary to control the proceedings to about the extent to which he does now. I favor that because otherwise I fear difficulties will develop due to groups of Indians within the tribe or within the nation, who are upset about something, and that the whole thing will be opened up to disorder and confusion, and possibly not only injustice to the attorneys of record but possibly injustice to many Indians as well. So a little further consideration, I hope, may be given to the language in the bill, with the idea of clarification. But cannot we consider that in executive session, Mr. Chairman? We will have these various amendments before us.

The CHAIRMAN. I was going to suggest to Judge Boudinot that if he would prepare his amendment in proper form and hand it to Mr. Grorud, we can consider it when we come to consider the bill in executive session.

Mr. BOUDINOT. That is all I want to bring to the attention of the committee, that it was only to protect the rights of the attorneys who have done work.

Senator STEIWER. They should be protected, but, Judge, would you not be just as satisfied if their status were preserved exactly as it is?

Mr. BOUDINOT. That is all.

Senator STEIWER. Retaining with the Secretary all the powers he now has?

Mr. BOUDINOT. Yes.

Senator STEIWER. An amendment to that general effect would do justice, would it not?

Mr. BOUDINOT. That is the intention. That is why I am here, and nothing else.

Mr. COLLIER. I am sure Mr. Case's amendment does cover it.

Senator STEIWER. We can consider them all further and probably arrive at a proper decision.

Mr. BOUDINOT. My criticism is that it falls too short. When it is once transferred, other attorneys can be gotten.

The CHAIRMAN. Mr. Blair, will you submit, if you care to, a revised text of lines 23, 24, and 25, on page 4, relating to the amount of weight certain reports shall have of the Commission?

Mr. BLAIR. I would be very glad to.

The CHAIRMAN. Submit the amendments to Mr. Grorud, and we will have them for our consideration when we come to consider this matter.

Mr. BLAIR. All right.

The CHAIRMAN. Mr. Stormont, have you any suggestions with regard to this bill?

Mr. STORMONT. Mr. Blair has a further suggestion, Mr. Chairman.

Mr. BLAIR. There is one matter that I feel perhaps it is incumbent upon me to bring to the attention of the committee. It is a matter about which I have no recommendation to make, but here is the situation:

I was called before a committee of the House a few weeks ago and asked about these cases in the Court of Claims. The committee requested that I draw up for that committee a form of bill providing that in all cases in the Court of Claims brought by Indian tribes gratuities should be allowed by the court. Complying with the committee's direction, of course, I did so. The committee seemed very much interested and insisted upon such general legislation.

In this bill there is no reference whatever to that subject. I bring the matter to the attention of this committee because that matter is being agitated, and it may be that the committee will care to consider some provision in the bill that this Commission shall, in making its reports to Congress, report what the records show with reference to gratuities, leaving it to the Congress to determine whether or not such gratuities shall be allowed.

As I say, I bring that to the committee merely as a matter of information, and not with any recommendation one way or the other.

SET-OFFS, COUNTERCLAIMS, GRATUITIES
STATEMENT OF CHARLES J. KAPPLER, ATTORNEY AT LAW, WASHINGTON, D. C.

Mr. Cairman, when Congressman (now Senator) Hayden, of Arizona, many years ago introduced the word " gratuities " in Indian jurisdictional bills, little did he, the members of both Indian committees, and of Congress itself, realize to what extremes the intent, purpose, and meaning of " gratuities " would be carried by the Court of

Claims, the Department of Justice, and the Comptroller General of the United States. Under the interpretation placed upon this word the Indian tribes have been compelled to reimburse the Government for expenses always considered governmental expenses incurred in carrying out the policies as well as the beneficial purposes of the United States, the benefits arising from which went primarily to the Government and only incidentally to the Indians. The Government reports from early days show that the pay of Indian agents, interpreters for such agents who were appointed to carry out treaty stipulations and keep the Government advised of the acts and intentions of Indians, expenses of delegations brought to Washington by the Government for the purpose of obtaining cessions of lands from them, and as several Indian commissioners have reported, to impress upon them how large and powerful this country was so as to imbue them with the idea it was useless to fight this great country; cost of transportation and insurance on annuity goods when the treaty or agreement with the Indians provided for the delivery of such annuity goods to the Indians on their reservation; and cost of educating and maintaining individual Indian children in nonreservation schools when their parents were overpersuaded and in some instances forced by General Pratt and his assistants to let the Government take their children to such nonreservation schools—all such expenditures have been embraced under the word gratuities. But the longest stretch of of interpretation was reached when it was adjudged that " presents " given to individual members of the tribe on visits to Washington in order to get into their good graces were included under the term " gratuities." On account of such all-embracing interpretation one bright Indian claims to have discovered the original " Injun-Giver " of our boyhood days, namely, " Uncle Sam."

Upon inquiry among a number of prominent members of the Indian committees of Congress, past and present, not one said that he had any idea that any of the items of expenditure above set forth would be charged to the Indians under the word " gratuities." It might not be amiss to say that Government attorneys before the Court of Claims were themselves most reluctant to assert against the Indians such set-offs or gratuities as presents.

In support of the statement that the items of expenditures above enumerated were always considered by the highest officials as made for and on behalf and for the benefit of the United States, the following is submitted:

PAY OF INDIAN AGENTS

Pay of Indian agents is not a proper set-off. The Court of Claims, in the *Fort Berthold case* (71 Ct. Cls. 305), speaking of education of Indian children at Government schools, held:

" The motive involved was more directly beneficial from a Government standpoint, to the Government than to the tribe."

Examination has been made in vain of Senate and House reports of committees on Indian jurisdictional bills and the debates in Congress for enlightenment as to what Congress had in mind as deductible items against awards made to Indians in the nature of set-offs, counterclaims, and gratuities. It is safe to assert, however, that no Senator or Congressman whose duties relate particularly to Indian affairs believed that pay of Indian agents was other than a governmental expenditure.

Acts of Congress defining duties of Indian agents show clearly their selection was never regarded as intended other than as a governmental instrumentality.

In the *Fort Berthold case*, above referred to, the court held:

" The sums chargeable, we think, must be restricted to the usually recognized and customary distributions made to the Indians as tribes and bands, unless a contrary purpose is expressed in the act."

The first general provision, aside from an act of May 19, 1796 (1 Stat. 469), for Indian agents is found in the act of March 30, 1802 (2 Stats. 139), section 13 of which provided:

" SEC. 13. That in order to promote civilization among the friendly Indian tribes, and *to secure the continuance of their friendship*, it shall be lawful for the President of the United States to cause them to be furnished with useful domestic animals, and implements of husbandry, and with goods and money, as he shall judge proper, and to appoint such persons, from time to time, as temporary agents to reside among the Indians as he shall think fit: *Provided*, That the whole amount of such presents and allowance to such agents shall not exceed $15,000 per annum."

Other provisions of this act show that a large part of the duties of the agent was to guard against Indian conflicts or wars, the agents, the employees, and the military affording to the Indians the protection and security of possession guaranteed to them by treaties, the act making it a criminal offense for white persons to hunt or range cattle on land " allotted or secured by treaty with the United States to any Indian tribes " and requiring travelers through Indian country to obtain permits from certain designated officials.

The act of June 30, 1834 (4 Stats. 729), continued this policy, with fuller and more definite field provisions due to the increasing extension of white settlement and travel. All employees in the Indian Service were placed under the direct supervision of the President or those nominated by him, and in no sense were they responsible or accountable to the Indian tribes.

These Indian agents were made agents of the United States to execute and perform the treaty obligations incumbent on the United States.

The act by section 11 provided that " payment of annuities or other sums stipulated by treaty shall be made to the chiefs of such tribe or to such persons as said tribe shall appoint."

Section 13 provided " * * * All purchases made on account of Indians and all payments to them of money or goods shall be made by *such person as the President may designate*. And the superintendent, agent, or subagent together with such military officer as the President may direct to be present, and certify to the *delivery of all goods and money required* to be paid or delivered to the Indians * * * and all persons charged with the disbursement or application of money, goods, or effects for the benefit of the Indians shall settle their account annually at the War Department."

Section 14 provided that " no persons employed in the Indian Department shall have any interest or concern in any trade with the Indians, except for and on account of the United States."

Interpreters were provided primarily for the benefit of the Indian agent and in order that he might communicate with those to whom he was sent and be better able to carry out treaty obligations. Without such an agent how could the Government carry out its treaty obligations?

The aforesaid act, by section 9, provided for interpreters and that their salary srould be $300 per year:

" That where there are different tribes at the same agency speaking different languages, one interpreter may be allowed for each of said tribes.   Interpreters shall be *nominated by the proper agents to the War Department* for approval * * * and in all cases where interpreters are employed for the *benefit of the Indians* preference shall be given to Indians."

This indicates the Government employed some interpreters for its use and others for use of Indians.

The duties of Indian agents and other Indian employees and that they were to perform service for the United States, and that the United States must be responsible for their salaries and expenses, were further defined as follows:

Revised Statutes, embodying act of July 29, 1848 (9 Stat. 264):

" SEC. 2147. The Superintendent of Indian Affairs and the Indian agents and subagents shall have authority to remove from the Indian country all persons found therein contrary to law, and the President is authorized to direct the military force to be employed in such removal.

" SEC. 2152. Superintendents, agents, and subagents shall endeavor to procure the arrest and trial of all Indians accused of committing any crime, offense, or misdemeanor, and of all other persons who may have committed crimes or offenses within any State or Territory and have fled to the Indian country either by demanding the same of the chiefs of the proper tribe or by such other means as the President may direct.

" SEC. 469. The Commissioner of Indian Affairs shall embody in his report the reports of all agents or commissioners issuing food, clothing, or supplies of any kind to Indians, stating the number of Indians present and actually receiving the same.

" SEC. 463. The Commissioner of Indian Affairs shall under the direction of the Secretary of the Interior and agreeably to such regulations as the President may prescribe, have the management of all Indian affairs and of all matters arising out of Indian relations."

Act of February 27, 1851 (9 Stats. 574):

" SEC. 3. That hereafter all Indian treaties shall be negotiated by such officers and agents of the Indian Department as the President may designate, and no officer or agent so employed shall receive additional compensation for such service."

The regulations as to Indian agents were in conformity with their obligation being to the United States.   The revised regulations of the Indian Service adopted June 1, 1837 (An. Rep. of Commissioner for 1837, p. 95), provided in part:

" GENERAL DUTIES OF AGENTS AND SUBAGENTS

" 5. To superintend and manage the intercourse of their respective tribes with other tribes and with citizens of the United States.

" 6. To carry into effect the instructions of the War Department or the Superintendent of Indian Affairs, and the regulations prescribed by the President.

" 7. To make and keep their agencies or subagencies within or near the tribes committed to their charge, at such points as the War Department shall designate, and not to depart from the limits of their agencies or subagencies without permission.

" PARTICULAR DUTIES

" Nominate to the Department suitable persons for teachers, blacksmiths, farmers, mechanics, etc.

"Agent or subagent will bind them, when appointed, by contracts to faithful performance of their duties.

"Agent and subagent will prepare and transmit annual statements covering farmers, mechanics, and others employed; the agricultural and other implements delivered to them and by them to the Indians, etc.

" Report number of each tribe and statements of what was done by teachers, farmers, etc.

"Agent will deliver to the smiths, millers, or farmers, the implements, iron, steel, coal, and other articles procured under treaty stipulation and taking receipts. Exercise supervision over them; visit the schools, make inspection of buildings, etc.

" With other provisions as to making of treaties, delivery of annuities, etc."

The annual report of the Commissioner of Indian Affairs for 1838, page 15, says:

" The powers and duties of agents and their permanent assignment to particular tribes are of long standing. The judiciousness of the latter, it is thought, may be well questioned. Referring not to personal considerations which are always dangerous ground of legislative or executive regulation, is it expedient to identify the agent with the tribe into which he is sent? Is there not some hazard of his becoming attached to their particular interests, to their customs, to leading men among them, to all that is theirs? The more there is in an agent to esteem, the more likely will it be to happen. * * * It is suggested whether it would not be better to allow each of them to reside but a limited time in any one district. By transferring them from one position to another, as frequently as may be regarded proper, they will be cut off from the strong enlistments of their feelings, or if perchance it will still occur, removal to another agency will produce kindred predilections elsewhere, and these attachments will neutralize each other."

Circular letter to Indian agents issued July 17, 1865:

" Your attention is called to the circular instruction from this office of January 26, 1865, in which the communication to the public of information of pending affairs relating to the Indians and a neglect to advise this office or the Interior Department of matters of importance, receiving or needing attention, was mentioned as being sufficient cause for dismissal from office.

    *   *   *   *   *   *

" If at any time it shall appear to you that officers of the Army are interfering with the proper execution of your duties *as civil agents of the Government*, or that they fail to render you such aid as is necessary to enable you to enforce regulations adopted alike for the good of the whites and Indians, you will content yourself with making a full representation of the facts at once to this office, or to the Secretary of the Interior, when measures will be taken by the Department to bring about if possible the cooperation of the military officers with you in such measures as may be deemed proper."

How well the agents frequently fulfilled their duties to the United States and to what extent they often regarded their assignment to the Indians as a commission to enrich themselves, in the old days, appears from the following extracts from the report of the Northwestern Treaty Commission, Newton Edmunds, chairman, to the Secretary of the Interior dated August 25, 1866:

" The apportionments to the tribes as they were ascertained from year to year, and the increase in prices and probable increase of fraudulent transactions, annually decreased the amounts received by some tribes, till the sum actually delivered was such a frivolous compensation for the time of waiting and distance traveled as to cause great dissatisfaction. Most of the tribes complained to us of this as unjust and unaccountable to them and your commissioners find it difficult to demonstrate to them the fidelity of the Government."

    *   *   *   *   *   *

" Indians are suspicious and comprehend frauds better than whites suppose, but they have been so remote from remedies and so ignorant of the means of redress, fraud has been perpetrated with such impunity as to be an established system of trade. Such things are not only pernicious, as they defraud either the Government or the Indians, but they disgust the Indian who comprehends and condemns them.

    *   *   *   *   *   *   *

"In the report which we and associates had occasion to make last fall we took the opportunity to call your attention to the flagrant and patent acts of negligence which had occurred in the administration of Indian Affairs, as exhibited to us on Indian territory . . . but our further progress up to more remote tribes has disclosed to us more mortifying evidence of negligence by former *agents*, and most probably stupendous frauds and outrages in the administration of Indian affairs which may deserve your special attention. Immediate arrangements should be made to place the present agents independent of traders. . . . Military officers should also be instructed to give attention to Government property and not, as in the instance referred to at Union, abandon a post, leaving $20,000 or $30,000 of Government goods uncared for."

*   *   *   *   *   *   *

"An Indian mark on a receipt is not sufficient evidence of anything. Without proper witnesses you have no assurance that he made it, and it is almost impossible to get one of those wild Indians to comprehend the meaning of his touching the pen.

*   *   *   *   *   *   *

"You have some good honest agents now in the administration of affairs, but our information admonishes us of the necessity of establishing a better system of vouchers to secure any permanent justice in the matter of Indian deliveries.

*   *   *   *   *   *   *

"Indians complained, and we think with justice, of the use of false weights, measures, and false-bottomed cups by traders and we unite with some of our commissioners who last year recommended some provision of law that will secure true measures and fair dealings among Indian tribes.

*   *   *   *   *   *   *

"It would be better for the Indians to deliver heavy articles at two or three different points as these prairie (blanket) Indians have no means of conveying or preserving heavy stores.

*   *   *   *   *   *   *

"Agents should be appointed in much greater numbers for the Indians of the Northwest. They should be located at military posts and in convenient communication with the tribes they superintend, and never as they have sometimes been years past, so far from their agencies as not to know the chiefs of the tribes or to be known by them. They should be in convenient and frequent communication with their people and not secluded and ignorant of the Indians for whom they *pretend* to be agents. (Annual Report Commissioner of Indian Affairs, 1866, p. 169.)"

Gen. John B. Sanborn, chairman of a commission to the Plains Indians, in a letter to the Secretary of the Interior dated October 23, 1865 (Ann. Rep. 1865, p. 536), said:

"They represent to us that they are neglected, poorly supplied, and cheated by their agent, Major Goodkins. That they are poorly supplied is evident from their appearance, and the residence of the agent is distant from the Indian camps 25 miles, and this distance the Indians are compelled to go for what supplies they receive."

The Commissioner's Report for 1875, page 23, says:

"I believe that the present unsatisfactory condition in which the Indians of this country are still found, notwithstanding the large and increasing outlays of money which the Government has been making for a half century, is due to the fact that by far the largest portion of the expenditures have been made with no practical reference to the question of civilization. An annuity in money or blankets, or bacon and beef, may have a tendency to draw the Indians within the reach of the Government and prepare them for the beginning of the work of civilization and also to *render them disinclined to take up arms and go upon the war path*. But with any tribe a few years of this treatment is sufficient for the purpose, and after this end has been gained a continuation of the feeding and clothing without a reference to further improvement on the part of the Indians is simply a waste of expenditure. This has been the case with a large portion of the money spent upon the Indians during the last 50 years. It is true that the letter of treaties may have been complied with by such expenditures and thus the credit of the Nation saved in form. But the spirit of the treaties which uniformly looked toward the civilization of the Indians has been disregarded in that no reasonable methods have been devised and adopted for promoting civilization.

   *   *   *   *   *   *   *

" Their (the Indians) own interests more strongly even than those of the Government require that they should be recognized and treated for what they are, an ignorant and helpless people who have a large moral claim upon the United States—a debt which cannot be discharged by gifts of blankets and bacon or any *routine official care* for their protection or relief."

In view of the official reports, is it just to charge them with the pay of agents of the United States?

PAY OF INTERPRETERS

The Commissioner of Indian Affairs' Annual Report for 1837, page 98, shows the regulations governing interpreters placed them directly under agents and required them to perform " any service that may be required of them " by agents.

The same report, page 6, says:

" The salaries of interpreters are too low. The best qualified persons cannot be obtained for them. They are engaged by traders and companies at rates of pay four times larger than those fixed by law. Yet *the intercourse with the Indians must be maintained through them.* The right understanding and successful issue of every negotiation depend upon their fidelity and ability. The fair representation of the wishes of the Indians to the Government, through their agents, is contingent upon their personal interests and biases. True policy demands that the compensation allowed for services of this character should be sufficient to remunerate capable men, and place them beyond the reach of temptation to do wrong."

The same report, page 53, report of H. R. Schoolcraft, says:

"Act to organize the Department. Nothing would improve and exalt the system of agencies more than raising the character of interpreters. We are dependent upon them for the most important communications to and from the Indians. The Government is liable to be accused of bad faith which may sometimes be owing to ignorance or unfaithfulness on the part of this class of persons. The ninth section of the act limits their annual pay to $300, which is so inadequate as to take from the Department those persons having a knowledge of the language who are best capacitated to serve them."

The commissioners' annual report for 1872, page 7, makes plain that both agents and interpreters were regarded as Federal and not Indian representatives. It says, speaking of the Indians:

" From their sense of wrongs suffered in the past and their suspiciousness arising from repeated acts of treachery on the part of the whites; from the great distance of many bands and individuals from points of personal communication with the *agents* of the Government, and the absence of all means of written communication with them; from the efforts of abandoned and degraded whites living among the Indians and exerting much influence over them, to misrepresent the policy of the Government and keep alive the hostility and suspicion of the savages; and *lastly* from the extreme untrustworthiness of many of the *interpreters* on whom the Government is obliged to rely for bringing *its intentions to* the knowledge of the Indians; that by the joint effort of all these obstacles many tribes and bands could come very slowly to hear, comprehend, and trust the professions and promises of the Government."

It is apparent from the foregoing that the salaries of agents, subagents, and interpreters were expenses of Government and are not proper subjects of set-offs.

Such expenses would seem not to be the subject of set-off or counter claim. The expenses so incurred are made by the United States for the benefit of the United States primarily, and if the Indians ever received anything therefrom it was merely incidental. The motive inducing the expenditure and, qui bono, for whose good, was thus succinctly expressed in the annual report of the Commissioner of Indian Affairs for 1837, page 5:

" It is believed that the visits of the several tribes to this city and to others upon the seaboard has had and will have a most salutary effect. So far as correct judgment can now be formed they will return to their kindred with just ideas of the strength and resources of the country, and of the friendly dispositions of our people toward them, and impressed with the conviction of the propriety of remaining at peace with *us* and with each other. Similar good results may be anticipated from the visits of the tribes who are expected to arrive next year."

Or the following from the annual report of the Commissioner for 1872, page 97:

" Several unusually large and important Indian delegations have visited Washington during the past year. The tribes represented and the personnel of the delegations may be characterized as follows:

" Red Cloud-Ogalalla Sioux: Delegation consisted of 30 Indians. * * * The Department in inviting the delegation was, however, more particularly influenced by the desire to impress the Ogalalla with the sense of the power of the Government, in view of the approach of the Northern Pacific Railroad to the rich hunting grounds of these Indians upon the Powder River. * * *

" Spotted Tails Band of Brule Sioux: This delegation consisted of 20 Indians. The object of inviting this delegation was to arrange amicably for the removal of the so-called ' Whetstone ' Agency * * * and also to confirm the friendship of the Brule Sioux toward the Government in view of the disaffection of the Ogalalla and the possibility of an early collision. The Indians gave a cordial assent to the wishes of the Department in respect of the removal of the agency, to which they had previously manifested their repugnance, and since their return have shown none but the best deposition toward the Government.

" Kiowas, Comanches, Apaches, Arapahoes, Wichitas, and affiliated bands: Largest and most conspicuous delegation ever brought to Washington, by H. E. Alvord, special commissioner for the pacification of these tribes. * * * The absence of the Cheyennes, who had been scared away from the place of meeting by the advance of Colonel McKenzie's force, and the refusal of the Quabada Comanches to send representatives to Washington constituted the only defects in the completeness and authority of the delegation."

This shows that the delegation came at the invitation of the United States, but some refused to come.

" The Grand River and Fort Peck Indians: This double delegation was brought to Washington by the commissioners who visited the upper Missouri for the pacification of the Sioux. * * * Their visit cannot fail to produce a decided effect by reducing the number of those who stand out against the progress of the railroad, even if it does not wholly withdraw the roving bands from their position of antagonism to the Government.

*　　　*　　　*　　　*　　　*　　　*　　　*

" The advantages of bringing well-constituted delegations from wild and potentially hostile tribes to Washington are very decided, and amply repay the expenditure involved. The impression derived thereby to the savages of the strength of the Government and the wealth and power of the whites is a more effective peacemaker than many soldiers, yet the *expenses of all the Indian delegations* that have visited Washington the last three years have *not equaled the cost of maintaining a company of cavalry for six months* in the field. * * * As it is at once cheaper and more humane to bring the savages to a realizing sense of their weakness and the impossibility of long contending with the Government, by giving a few chiefs and braves *free* rides on our railroads and Broadway omnibuses than by surprising their camps on winter nights and shooting down men, women, and children together in the snow."

How unjust to charge the Indian tribes for such expenses which the Government incurred for individuals and repeated the benefit!

The authority for bringing delegations to Washington or other points and for giving presents and provisions to the Indians is to be found in the act approved May 13, 1800 (2 Stat. 85), which authorizes the President to issue rations in his judgment and as can be spared from the Army to Indians who may visit military posts on the frontiers or within their respective nations. Other sections provide:

" SEC. 2. That the President of the United States shall be further authorized to cause to be defrayed, on the part of the United States, the reasonable expenses of such Indians as may from time to time visit the seat of government thereof, for their journeys to, stay at, and return from the same; and also cause to be given such Indians during their stay such presents as he shall judge necessary.

" SEC. 3. That a separate account of all rations issued and expenses defrayed as aforesaid and of the expenditures occasioned by such presents as aforesaid, shall be kept at the Department of War."

This policy had its precedents in the acts of Sir Walter Raleigh in North Carolina and of Oglethorpe of Georgia, who (Terhune's Life of Oglethorpe), as English governor of Savannah and Georgia in 1734, " made friends with the Indians, even taking their chiefs to England on a visit."

The annual report of the Commissioner of Indian Affairs for 1872, page 4, thus states the Government's view before Indian jurisdictional acts were passed:

" It is hardly less absurd on the first view of it that delegations from tribes that have frequently defied our authority and fought our troops, and have never yielded more than a partial and grudging obedience to the most reasonable requirements of the Government, should be entertained at the national capital, feasted, and loaded with presents. * * * And yet, for all this, the Government is right and its critics wrong; and the 'Indian policy' is sound, sensible, and beneficent, because it reduces to the minimum the loss of life and property upon the frontier and allows the freest development of our settlements and railways possible under the circumstances.

* * * * * * *

" It will be sufficient, perhaps, to mark the distinction to say that a general Indian war could not be carried on with the present military force of the United States, or anything like it. Regiments would be needed where now are only companies, and long lines of posts would have to be established for the protection of regions which, under the safeguard of the feeding system, are now left wholly uncovered. On the other hand, by the reservation system and the feeding system combined the occasions for collision are so reduced by lessening the points of contact and the number of Indians available for hostile expeditions involving hardship, exposure, and danger, is so diminished through the appeal made to their indolence and self-indulgence that the Army in its present force is able to deal effectively with the few marauding bands which refuse to accept the terms of the Government."

From the foregoing it is evident that the expenses of delegations should not come within any definition of counterclaim or set-off, legal or equitable. As the real underlying and fundamental purpose was benefit to the United States, and very frequently if not usually, the procurement of a treaty with accompanying land cessions from the Indians, such expenditures should not be classed as set-offs against the Indians. As stated in *State* v. *Cincinnati Southern*

R. R. (248 U. S. 26–29), a " grant of right-of-way for a railroad from which the public is to receive great benefits is not a gratuity within the constitutional provisions against ' gratuities ' from public funds."

Such expenditures were rather part of the Federal overhead than charges to be made against the Indians.

TUITION AT NONRESERVATION SCHOOLS

These expenses are prorated charges against the Indian tribes for costs of buildings and support and maintenance of Indian nonreservation schools at Carlisle, Haskell, Chilocco, Pierre, and Pipestone. The expenditures were not made pursuant to any treaty and cannot be construed as a compliance with any treaty requirement. These institutions were established by the United States Government pursuant to a general Federal scheme for advancement of Indians. The pupils received were individuals. It is wholly an individual affair, and Indian parents consented on the urgent solicitation of General Pratt, superintendent, and other Government officials to permit their children to leave the reservation to attend such schools. Such items would not appear to be within the contemplation of set-offs under any jurisdictional act as money expended for the benefit of the " *tribes or bands.*" It could hardly be contended that when States or cities have established public schools for the children residing in said States or cities, such States and cities would be chargeable with additional expense in the event parents sent their children to colleges for a higher education than was afforded in such public schools.

TRANSPORTATION—INSURANCE

The legal question involved covering set-off for transportation, insurance, and so forth, is, Where an Indian treaty provides for delivery not in annual sums of money, but payments to the sum stated to be made in kind, such as goods, merchandise, and so forth, is the amount stated inclusive or exclusive of cost of transportation and insurance? Immemorial custom has been that the United States should pay the cost of transportation, insurance, and so forth. Delivery was to be at the agency of the Indians. The Government's obligation was not met until delivery was made. The Government was under contract to make delivery, and in order to insure delivery it incurred insurance charges solely for its own benefit.

There is nothing in any jurisdictional act to warrant a holding that the transportation charges of fulfilling a treaty obligation was upon the Indians. Indeed, the United States forbade the Indians to travel outside of their reservation except with express permission.

The Supreme Court has held that a departure from custom dealing with Indians is not lightly to be inferred when it comes to construction of Indian treaties. And the statutes also evidence the intention that the transportation charges should be borne by the United States. Therefore transportation, insurance, etc., charges when claimed as set-offs are not proper off-sets, but a legal liability of the United States.

The fact that the United States always has borne the costs of transportation and has treated the same as exclusive of the treaty amounts stipulated to be paid brings the case within the rule of *United States* v. *Nice* (241 U. S.   7) :

According to a familiar ruling, legislation affecting the Indians is to be construed in their interest, and a purpose to make a radical departure is not likely to be inferred.

PRESENTS

The act of May 13, 1800 (2 Stat. 85), expressly provided that the President should use Government funds to pay for presents for the Indians. No subsequent act has been passed by Congress expressly providing that money expended by the Government for presents to Indians should be reimbursed the Government by the Indians receiving such presents. Under the act of 1800 while delegations were visiting the President or officials at Washington it was customary to give them each a present when the members were ready to return home. These presents represented a small tribute from the President to these wild people as a mark of appreciation, which presents the individuals would forever keep. How this great Government, after having voluntarily given such presents and the Indians themselves in numerous instances having given presents to the officials in return, can now demand payment for such presents from the tribe, not from the individuals to whom such presents were given, is astounding. At most, the present was an individual personal matter, and to demand them back or payment therefor would make Uncle Sam appear most ungracious. A voluntary gift to individual Indians cannot be classed as legal set-offs as against the tribe which received no benefit whatever from such gifts. It should be remembered that chiefs and delegations of Indian tribes brought with them gifts to be given the President and officials of the Government. We have yet to hear of a case where such gifts were demanded back by the Indians. Furthermore, Congress in providing in a jurisdictional act for set-offs and gratuities to be charged against any money award to the Indians had in mind legal set-offs and donations of money or goods for the benefit of the tribe as a whole, not mere gifts to a few Indians for their personal adornment or for keepsakes.

In order to avoid further injustices of this character being perpetrated upon the Indian tribes, it is respectfully submitted that an amendment to the pending bill reading on the lines following should be inserted therein:

That the said Indian Commission shall construe the terms " counterclaims and set-offs " as meaning such counterclaims and set-offs as are defined by principles of law and rules of equity; and the terms " gratuities " and " money expended for the benefit of any such tribe or band of Indians " as embracing the actual cost of annuity goods, livestock, implements, etc., furnished to and money expended for the sole and direct benefit of any such tribe or band of Indians by the United States beyond treaty or agreement or act of Congress stipulations; and as excluding pay of United States Indian superintendents, agents, subagents, and interpreters; expenses of delegations of Indians when called to Washington at the instance of the Government; cost of presents given to members of such delegations by the Government; cost of transportation of and insurance on annuity goods, livestock, implements, etc., when a treaty or agreement or act of Congress provided for the delivery of such annuity goods, etc., to the Indians on their reservation; and cost of educating and maintaining individual Indian children in Government noreservation schools: *Provided*, That this provision shall apply as well to Indian claim cases now pending before the Court of Claims as to those which Congress may hereafter refer to said court or over which the Indian Commission herein provided for shall have jurisdiction.

MEMORANDUM SUBMITTED BY RUFUS G. POOLE, ASSISTANT SOLICITOR, DEPARTMENT OF THE INTERIOR, REGARDING THE PROPOSED AMENDMENT DEFINING COUNTERCLAIMS, SET-OFFS, AND GRATUITIES TO THE INDIAN CLAIMS COMMISSION BILL, S. 2731

The proposed amendment, which attempts to define counterclaims, set-offs, and gratuities in connection with claims presented to the Claims Commission to be created under S. 2731, is considered by the Solicitor's staff to be undesirable and inappropriate for the following reasons:

1. The amendment purports to define words which are not used in the bill, except for the word "set-offs", which appears on line 10, page 4, of the bill.

2. The definition to be attributed to the words "counterclaims and set-offs" is so vague as to have no meaning. There exist no principles of law or rules of equity defining counterclaims and set-offs. If reference is intended to cases on the subject it is notable that the opinions of the Court of Claims differ repeatedly on this subject. Expenditures which are in some cases held not to be counterclaims or set-offs are in later cases treated in an opposite manner.

3. The proposed definition of gratuity is entirely too detailed to be appropriate as legislation. Legislation should deal with matters in a general way, setting out fields for action, and should not attempt to list every conceivable eventuality. It would be a dangerous policy to enumerate all possible gratuities, as is attempted here, since it would be inevitable that some subjects would be excluded or misplaced. Furthermore, such an enumeration would operate as a strait-jacket upon the Commission and would prevent the exercise of its discretion in particular cases.

4. The language of the bill as it now reads would allow for a wide exercise of discretion on the part of the Commission in determining set-offs in individual cases; but, even more important, it would allow the Commission to set out standards on the basis of its familiarity with the problem as to what should be and what should not be treated as set-offs. The allowance of such freedom is one of the most important provisions of the bill, and its curtailment would jeopardize the value of the Commission. It must be borne in mind that the work of the Commission will be reported to Congress, and Congress should have the benefit of the determinations of the Commission made according to its best discretion in the light of the facts as they may appear during the course of its research.

———

DEPARTMENT OF JUSTICE,
Washington, June 20, 1935.

Mr. GRORUD: This definition (proposed amendment defining "gratuities", and "set-offs" submitted by Mr. Kappler) seems all right with two exceptions:

First. "Costs of educating and maintaining Indian children in Government nonreservation schools" is excepted from gratuities. In some claims, a treaty has provided that the Government would erect and maintain schools on the reservations for Indian children. Instead of doing this the Government has sent the children to nonreservation schools and thus the children have really gotten what the treaty called for, i. e., an education.

If this definition is adopted, the tribes can sue the Government on their claim for failure to comply with the treaty provisions as to school, and the Government would be unable to offset against that portion of the claim the actual moneys that have been actually spent for giving the children the education which was the purpose of the treaty in the first place. I therefore think this part of the definition should be changed.

Second. "The pay of United States Indian superintendents, agents, subagents and interpreters" should not be excluded, because this is an expense which the court has held is directly for the benefit of the tribes concerned.

Faithfully yours,

HARRY W. BLAIR,
Assistant Attorney General.

The CHAIRMAN. If there is no further suggestion regarding the bill, the hearings on S. 2731 will be concluded. As soon as we have the amendments in the hands of the committee, the committee in executive session will proceed to pass upon the amendments.

(Thereupon, at 11:20 a. m., the committee adjourned sine die.)